Empowerm

James O'Heare

Title: Empowerment Training 2nd Edition

Publisher: BehaveTech Publishing, Ottawa Canada.

www.BehaveTech.com

Author: James O'Heare

Cover art and book design: James O'Heare

Copy Editor: Kamrin MacKnight

ISBN 978-1-927744-23-9

for Pascale, my loving wife.

Preface

In this book, I explore a range of circumstances and behavioral phenomena represented by the word "empowerment." I also discuss some training strategies and practices that promote and prevent empowerment. These applies to any species of animal, including, more or less, humans. Finally, I discuss the rehabilitation of disempowerment, again empowerment and disempowerment representing a number of related conditions or patterns of behavior.

Empowerment is not something typically addressed by a scientist because it is one of those airy-fairy, colloquial, and pseudoscientific notions that most scientists would not take seriously. Words like empowerment and disempowerment, though commonly utilized in rather unscientific terms, tact certain kinds of real behavioral phenomena and stripped of their mystical trappings could potentially be useful. Most scientists under such contingencies might opt to explore the real behavioral phenomena without invoking baggage-laden colloquial terms. On the other hand, the term "empowerment" does evoke a unique set of verbal behaviors that more technical terms do not seem adequate to cover in one word or phrase. The concept of empowerment calls attention to certain clusters of circumstances that are rarely identified in the very specific functional behavioral analysis and functional diagnostic processes within behaviorology.

For these reasons, I entertain the term in this book, as least in as much as it evokes said attention and makes proper analysis more likely. However, my entertaining the term extends only far enough to identify a range of issues to be explored. The concept of empowerment is intriguing because it tends to be evoked under contingencies involving a number of real problems and their solutions, that, if treated more seriously, could potentially benefit a great many persons (be they human or otherwise). Personally, the word empowerment evokes private verbal behaviors (i.e., thoughts and chains of thoughts) related to a number of actual situations that are of interest to bettering lives, including response depression, conditioned helplessness, and excessive aversive emotional arousal. My objective is to explore all of the related issues, but to do so in a more scientifically sound manner than has been typical of the concept, including in the now quite old first edition of this book.

I will assume a professional audience of behaviorologists, behavior analysts, animal trainers, and behavior technologists, and hence a basic familiarity with the foundational principles of behavior and specific animal training techniques. However, as I proceed, I review some of these principles and procedures as they relate to empowerment training tactics. I use proper technical terminology for the purposes of clarity and precision, but I also attempt to define the terms as they are introduced. For further information on key terms, please refer to the Encyclopedic Glossary of Terms of the Association of Animal Behavior Professionals (see list of resources at the end of the book). Readers who are less experienced with the principles of behavior might start by reading my book *Problem Animal Behavior.*

Many of the topics I discuss are far from conclusively established—another part of the problem in tackling this topic. It is important to remember while reading, that there is controversy regarding some of these issues. This is particularly true of some theories accounting for observed behavioral phenomena. In many cases, the phenomena are well known and readily predicted but the hypothesized mechanisms underlying them are not. For instance, we frequently speak of "learned helplessness" and "systematic desensitization," but these notions involve not only the readily observable phenomena but also hypothesized explanations for them that are still debated. This should not stop us from discussing these matters. I generally attempt to stick to the effects and forgo in-depth discussion of the theories attempting to account for them, but this is not always be possible. Where I discuss the theories, I either present the hypothesis that seems to be favored or discuss different plausible perspectives.

This book makes use of a number of published reports of research on non-human animals, that are repugnant and outrageous. I have and continue to struggle with whether to write a book that presents the results from such research. I have chosen to do so because it is already done and the findings may indeed help others. However, I am loath to reinforce such research by describing and citing it. I attempt to offset this harm by being absolutely clear and frank here in this preface regarding my stance on the topic. It is a mad world indeed, where learning more about some phenomenon (such as what happens when you deprive an infant of their mother or expose animals to inescapable intense electric shocks or drop rats into water and see how long it takes them to give up and die under different situations) is considered adequate justification for causing extreme and persistent pain and suffering, and indeed ruining lives and even killing. I do not condone experimentation on non-human animals that requires any kind of exploitation, which includes keeping them in captivity, regardless of whether the experiment causes physical or behavioral harm as well and regardless of how "valuable" anyone believes the results to be. Non-human animals cannot provide informed consent. As a rule of thumb, if an experiment and everything that conducting it requires would not be acceptably carried out on young children (with or without parental consent), then it would be no more acceptable to carry it out on a non-human.

This is a work in progress. Once it is published, I will surely continue to hone and develop my treatment of the topic, so that it will evolve over time. I will prepare new editions of this book to improve the idea of empowerment training. Consider this book an approximation, with the terminal approximation to be shaped into a form as yet unknown.

Table of Contents

Introduction

Empowerment is one of those new-age words beloved among self-help gurus, psychologists, other pseudoscientists, and lay persons, and avoided by scientists. However, the term "empowerment" tends to be evoked under circumstances that could potentially be examined scientifically. It has been argued to me that the term comes with so much pseudoscientific baggage that it is likely best to avoid it. However, the word is commonly appreciated by a non-scientist audience. I use the word "empowerment" in this book to represent a number of related behavioral phenomena, including conditioned helplessness, response depression, excessive risk aversion or flight, excessive emotionality, and self-mutilative or other destructive displacement activities. I attempt to provide a reasonably useable definition for "empowerment," something that ties many of these concepts together. The term "empowerment" is used as an umbrella term, the lack of which represents a number of impediments to adaptive behavioral well-being. I discuss these behavioral phenomena and explore how this might suggest practical applications to help resolve certain kinds of problematic patterns of behavior or to avoid these problems.

First, I provide a brief introduction to some elementary principles of behavior that ought to inform any behavior change project. Next, I explore the concept of empowerment, and related concepts, attempting to define it in terms that are scientific and might inform practical applications. Finally, I attempt to bring the coverage together with practical tips on preventing or resolving problems that might evoke the term "disempowerment."

But first, I elaborate the difference between scientific and non-scientific approaches and disciplines since the whole point of this book is to take a topic that is commonly framed in non-scientific terms and reframe it in scientific terms. Many fields of study examine behavior-related phenomena, and each is distinguished by a particular set of postulates, initial assumptions and/or objectives. Psychology, for instance, emphasizes the hypothetical construct "mind," which is said to "choose" or "decide" how the body will conduct itself, more or less semi-autonomously of nature. The discipline tends to focus on tracing behavior back to the free-willing choices of this inner behavior-initiating agent, which it considers the "underlying cause" of the behavior. Efforts to change behavior are usually directed at convincing the "mind" to "choose" to change via "will." Psychology meets the definition of a pseudoscience because, while it utilizes some scientific words and some scientific methods, it does not adhere to the assumptions of natural science, commonly known by the public as just "science."

Behaviorology is the natural science of environment–behavior functional relations, completely independent of the pseudoscience, psychology. Natural science (aka "science") is an empirical approach to studying phenomena of nature based on certain philosophical assumptions that together go by the name "naturalism." Naturalism is a philosophy of science, utilized by all natural sciences, which holds that *only natural events exist, there are no non-real or non-natural events, and all natural events are theoretically measurable in terms of mass, time, distance, temperature, and/or charge*. Natural scientists simply do not study proposed non-natural or supernatural events; nor may they postulate them as part of an explanation for natural events. If a supposed event is not at least theoretically measurable, it is not natural, and not an appropriate topic of study. It is only through careful adherence to these assumptions and constraints that natural science can generate such robust, reliable products (such as space shuttles, vaccines, massive skyscrapers, and personal computers) when compared to other, less stringently constrained (i.e., mystical) methods of studying nature.[1] Clark (2007) put it eloquently: "To be a thorough-going naturalist is to accept yourself as an entirely natural phenomenon. Just as science shows no evidence for a supernatural god "up there," there's no evidence for an immaterial soul or mental agent "in here," supervising the body and brain."

---

[1] By comparison, for example, psychology is notoriously ineffective at explaining behavior and even less effective in controlling behavior. Likewise, astrology fails to generate effective predictions of behavior.

This book presents a behaviorology perspective. There is no speculation about what animals may or may not understand, desire, or want, or what might be occurring inside a so-called "mind" between stimulation and their behavior. There is no discussion of other fictitious constructs such as "dominance." Nor do I label problem behaviors with names to provide supposed explanation for them. Instead, the focus of this book is on the actual functional relations of which the behaviors of concern are a part.

Chapter 1. Foundational Principles of Behavior

Introduction

This *very* basic introduction to the foundational principles of behavior will help put errorless differential added reinforcement procedures in context and provide a review of concepts that professionals should already be familiar with and which arise in discussion of applying errorless differential added reinforcement to cases.

Types of Behavior

There are two fundamentally distinct kinds of behavior. ***Operant behaviors*** are behaviors maintained by the consequences that follow it. Operant behaviors include sitting, walking, talking, biting, growling, and even thinking. ***Respondent behavior*** is innate behavior that is insensitive to consequences. Respondent behavior occurs "reflexively," as biologists put it. Respondent behaviors occur because the organism has evolved to exhibit such "reflexive" behaviors when an eliciting stimulus is presented, regardless of what stimulation might follow it. Respondent behaviors include salivating when food is presented, blinking when a puff of air or dirt touches the eyeball, sneezing when the nasal cavity is tickled, retracting the hand when touching a hot stove, and emotional behaviors (emotional behaviors involve the release of chemicals into the bloodstream by glands and certain accompanying neural processes).

Let's explore a number of more specific terms related to behavior. Whereas the term ***behavior*** is generic, a ***response*** is a particular occurrence of a behavior. No two responses will ever be precisely the same in every way.

Thus, a response is a one-time event. By definition, one cannot repeat a one-time event and therefore we cannot track it quantitatively (except to say that one event occurred). If drinking in general is an example of a behavior, drinking on one particular occasion is a response.

When we are under contingencies to identify a number of functionally related responses, usually so that we may identify instances of their occurrence and count them, a way is needed to define sets of functionally related responses. The concept of a "response class" resolves this problem. A ***response class*** refers to a set of individual responses that share a common eliciting stimulus (for respondent behaviors, discussed below), or consequential effect on the environment (for operant behaviors). If a number of operant behaviors are maintained by the same outcome (i.e., reinforcer), they are members of the same operant response class—these operant behaviors are ***functionally equivalent*** (although they are not necessarily topographically equivalent).

As we explore in greater detail below, an ***operant behavior*** is behavior that is influenced by consequences. An ***operant response class***, as a set of behaviors, may differ topographically (i.e., appear different), but the behaviors share a common effect on the environment (i.e., the consequence). That is, members of an operant response class share in common, not how they look or sound etc., but the consequence they generate. The concept of a response class allows us to categorize and analyze iterations of functionally equivalent responses over time.

We are often under contingencies to refer to the member responses within a response class, and for that the phrase "response class members" is used. ***Response class members*** are simply responses within a response class.

Let's say that we are under contingencies to specify a form (topography) of interest within the context of functionally equivalent responses—that is, defining it by some criterion that relates to how the behavior appears (i.e., looks, sounds, feels etc.), or otherwise how it is topographically exhibited. In many cases, an entire response class is a problem—that is, any form that it takes is a problem. But, in many cases, the problem is not the shared outcome, but rather how that outcome is generated. In other words, some forms of the response class are acceptable and other forms are not. In these kinds of cases, we need a mechanism by which to define specific forms within a response class. For example, in consuming water, chug-a-lugging might be a problematic form whereas sipping is not. A ***response class form*** is a set of responses within a response class that share a specific topographic feature or criterion. Within the response class of drinking, we might define chug-a-lugging as our behavior of concern. We could define this by the liquid being consumed from a container in large gulps in rapid succession, maintaining contact with the container between gulps. This then is the response class form of concern, which separates that form within the response class from all other forms that drinking might take, and we might call this "chug-a-lugging" for conciseness. This allows us to determine when, among any number of behaviors, this response class form occurs and does not occur. We can therefore count them and calculate the rate or relative frequency over time, which will inform us regarding the strength of that behavior. This in turn, allows us to set goals regarding changing the strength of the behavior and to compare the strength of the behavior before and after an intervention.

Causes of Behavior

The environment causes behavior—in the case of operants, something occurs immediately before a behavior that evokes it. That stimulus evokes the behavior because there has been a history of that stimulus → behavior contingency being immediately followed by another stimulus that has reinforced that stimulus → behavior functional relationship. Let us explore the concept of contingencies and functional relationships so that we may better appreciate what causes operant behaviors.

The Three-Term Contingency (aka the ABCs of Behaviorology)

To better understand what causes behavior (and hence what we must do to change behavior), the three-term contingency must be appreciated. The three-term contingency is sometimes referred to as the "ABCs of behaviorology," and it can be useful to frame the three-term contingency concept this way for clients. The three-term contingency is the basic starting point formula for analyzing episodes of behavior, which is necessary when devising an intervention to resolve problematic behaviors.

"A" stands for "antecedent," which means before the behavior. "B" stands for "behavior." "C" stands for "consequence." Both A and C represent stimulation and B is, of course, the behavior in question. By understanding what evokes a behavior and what reinforces the behavior, that is, the functional relationship between the behavior and the stimulation causing it, we understand *why* the behavior occurs and this helps suggest what we can change in order to change the behavior. We do not change behavior (B) directly but rather make changes to what causes it (A and C). The relationship between A and B and between B and C are referred to as "functional relations" and the terms (i.e., A, B, and C) plus the functional relations between them are referred to as "contingencies." Let us examine the three-term contingency more closely.

The three-term contingency is depicted this way: A → B → C. The arrows (e.g., →) indicate a functional relation. Once it is determined that A evokes the behavior, we refer to that antecedent stimulus as an ***evocative stimulus*** (S^{Ev}). Thus, the conditioning of operant behaviors requires at least a three-term (evocative stimulus → behavior → consequence) contingency of the general stimulus–response–stimulus form. Thus, the evocative stimulus *functionally controls* the behavior, which in turn, *functionally controls* the consequence.

Another component of the antecedent environment is the ***function-altering stimulus*** (S^{FA}), which is any antecedent stimulus that does not evoke the behavior but rather alters the nervous system of the subject and thereby alters the capacity of the evocative stimulus to evoke the behavior. An important type of function-altering stimulus is the ***motivating operation*** (MO). The motivating operation (like other S^{FA}) comes before the evocative stimulus in contingency diagrams. The motivating operation does not evoke behavior but rather temporarily influences the effectiveness of stimuli as reinforcers (i.e., the "value-altering" effect), which makes the evocative stimulus more or less likely to evoke the behavior (i.e., the behavior-altering effect).

Take note that contingencies are brief events. A stimulus will evoke a behavior right away and not later, and if a consequence occurs more than within a few seconds of the behavior, it will not influence the rate of that behavior.

Conditioning

Conditioning is a behavior change process involving an enduring change in behavior due to experience. Conditioning is a biological process that occurs within the subject's body, most notably within the nervous system. There are two fundamentally different kinds of conditioning that correspond to the two fundamental types of behavior.

Operant conditioning is a behavior change process whereby a behavior becomes more or less likely to occur on subsequent occasions as a result of the consequences that the operant behavior has generated. Some kinds of consequences result in an *increase* in the likelihood of the behavior occurring again and some result in a *decrease* in their likelihood. The different types of operant conditioning are explored below. The key feature of operant conditioning is that the likelihood of the behavior changes as a result of consequences.

Respondent conditioning is a behavior change process whereby a stimulus that previously did not elicit a respondent behavior is paired with a stimulus that does, and as a result, the neutral stimulus also comes to elicit the respondent behavior. Respondent conditioning does not involve consequences but rather the expansion of what will elicit the respondent behavior.

Our emphasis is generally on operant behaviors, as these are most commonly the behavior we seek to change. However, the role of respondent conditioning is considered where it impacts upon the operant behaviors of concern.

The Three-Term Contingency in Detail

Antecedent Stimulus (A)

The antecedent stimulus category of most interest is the evocative stimulus. The ***evocative stimulus*** is the stimulus that evokes the behavior and it occurs immediately before the behavior. All operant behavior is evoked—it is just a matter of identifying which, among any number of things happening right before the behavior actually evokes it. This can be tested experimentally by isolating stimulus features and presenting them independently of one another, noting which actually changes the rate of the behavior.

The evocative stimulus is usually, but not always, obvious. For example, someone approaches the dog and he scurries away or he growls and snarls and then if the person approaches closer, he snaps at them or bites. Or, thunder occurs and the dog begins to tremble, pace, and whine. Or, the dog is left alone and he begins to pace, dig at door-jambs, howl, and bark. In most cases, as the contingency is repeated, we can note that one stimulus is always present and that stimulus is usually the evocative stimulus. Sometimes, it is difficult to identify exactly what evokes the behavior. For example, dogs might be playing, or otherwise interacting amiably and they usually do, except that sometimes, one of the dogs will suddenly attack the other dog and no obvious common denominator is readily identifiable. This kind of situation often involves a complex arrangement of evocative stimuli and difficult to detect function-altering stimuli. Functional analysis experiments can often be carried out to tease out and test different hypotheses, but this is also not always easy and sometimes not safe to carry out.

It is important to specifically and objectively describe stimuli. If the dog reacts when anyone waves their arms in the air above their head, then it is important to identify exactly and precisely that action, rather than any vague terms like people "getting excited" or "making a fuss," or any number of other phrases that might be taken to mean different things to different people. Your identification of evocative stimuli should describe actual movements or energy changes rather than broad characterizations of events.

Behavior (B)

Behavior is any measurable, neurally-mediated reaction of a body part to stimulation. The reaction might be neuromuscular or solely neural. In other words, it can involve the externally noticeable movements of body parts by innervated muscles, or it can be solely neural, including consciousness-related behaviors (e.g., those behaviors commonly referred to as thinking, recognizing, comprehending, and/or visualizing) and observable only to the individual exhibiting the behavior. Private behaviors such as these are behaviors because they are directly observable and measurable, even if just to an audience of one—the organism exhibiting the behavior. They are not, however, observable to others and so when analyzing the behavior of others, it is appropriate to target observable and measurable behaviors for analysis.

The word "reaction," as opposed to some other word such as "response," highlights the reactive and passive (rather than active and initiative) nature of behavior, in that behavior is fully caused and not autonomously initiated by a supposed inner-agent without physical status that may "will" the body to act independent of the laws of nature. Behavior is simply the body's reaction to stimulation. In beings with a nervous system, we call this "behavior."

Emotional responses are real behaviors (of the respondent type, as opposed to operant), involving the release of chemicals into the bloodstream by glands and certain accompanying neural processes. This important topic is discussed further below in the context of changing emotional behaviors.

The three-term contingency relates to operant behaviors specifically (respondent contingencies are quite different and are composed of two terms rather than three). ***Operant behavior*** is behavior that is influenced by consequences. If a behavior can be reinforced or punished, then it is operant behavior. Respondent behaviors are not susceptible to consequences and their conditioning occurs differently, which is why we make this important distinction.

It is also important to distinguish between traits or characterizations and behaviors. Some people may describe an animal's behavior as "stubbornness," "rudeness," "spitefulness," "selfishness," "aggression," "hostility," or "fearful," and although these descriptors might satisfy a general verbal characterization of a pattern of behavior, they are not clearly defined behaviors *per se*. In analyzing behavior, it is vital to identify the function and often the form of the behavior itself. When defining a behavior for the sake of your contingency analysis, be specific and precise. Avoid vague or ambiguous terms. In all cases, your target behavior definition should define just the problematic behaviors and not include similar behaviors.

Consequence (C)

A consequence is any event (a) immediately following a behavior, (b) is generated by that behavior, and (c) changes the rate or relative frequency of the behavior in the future. There are a number of types of consequences, defined by whether the stimulus is *added* to the situation or *subtracted* from it and whether it subsequently *increases* or *decreases* in rate or relative frequency of the behavior.

Operant Conditioning

How Conditioning Occurs

As described above, operant conditioning is a behavior change process whereby a behavior becomes more or less likely to occur on subsequent occasions as a result of the consequences generated by the operant behavior.[2] In an operant three-term contingency, there are two 2-term contingencies, which are integrally related in a way that generates operant conditioning. The behavior → consequence contingency strengthens or weakens the antecedent → behavior functional relationship, resulting in an increase or decrease in the likelihood of the behavior when the subject is faced with the evocative stimulus again. Throughout our lives, our behavior repeatedly generates consequences, which may change from occasion to occasion and the behavior becomes more and less likely over time based on these experiences. Stimuli come to evoke operant behaviors or not, based on the kinds of consequences that have followed that behavior in the past. This is not something we initiatively "choose"—all behavior is completely caused by the environment in the way described above, even though due to our ignorance with respect to the distant links in the chain of causes, we might sometimes feel otherwise.

Also as described above, contingencies are temporally brief events. The evocative stimulus can only evoke behaviors immediately and consequences will only influence the rate of behavior if they occur during or within a few seconds of the behavior finishing—and the sooner it occurs, the more effective it will be. This is called "***contiguity***." There is another important variable in determining the effectiveness of conditioning, which is called "contingency." Don't be confused by this related use of the word "contingency." In this context, ***contingency*** refers to the degree of the functional relationship between the behavior and the consequence. Highly contingent consequences only occur following the behavior in question and occur each time that the behavior occurs. The higher the degree of contingent

[2] The reiteration of definitions and concepts is "intentional" and contributes to conditioning a higher degree of fluency in their use by the reader.

consequences, the more effective will be those consequences. Behavior can be maintained with moderate contingency, meaning that the behavior is reinforced sometimes, but not necessarily every time and the reinforcer in question can be contacted sometimes outside of the contingency in question.

Types of Operant Conditioning Processes

Operant conditioning can be divided into different types. Consider Figure 1. Notice the two dimensions of *added* versus *subtracted* consequences and *increased* versus *decreased* likelihood of responding in the future.

Responding **Increases**

Consequence **Added**

Added Reinforcement **+R**	Subtracted Reinforcement **-R**
Added Punishment **+P**	Subtracted Punishment **-P**

Consequence **Subtracted**

Responding **Decreases**

Figure 1. Table of Consequences.

Figure 1 illustrates four primary principles of behavior and types of operant conditioning. These include added reinforcement (+R), subtracted reinforcement (–R), added punishment (+P), and subtracted punishment (–P). The type of conditioning is determined by whether the consequence was *added* to or *subtracted* from the situation and by whether the behavior subsequently *increases* or *decreases* in likelihood. To analyze any instance of a change in the rate or relative frequency of operant behavior, determine whether the consequence in any given trial was added or subtracted and whether the behavior subsequently increased or decreased. This provides the data to determine under which principle the contingency operated. An analysis of repeated trials will provide an indication of the course of that change and which principle predominates. Let's consider each type in turn.

Reinforcement

Reinforcement is a behavior change process in which a change in stimulation, during or immediately following a response, results in an increase in the likelihood of the behavior on subsequent occasions. The behavior → reinforcer contingency results in a *strengthening* of the evocative stimulus → behavior functional relation. On subsequent occasions of its occurrence, the evocative stimulus is *more* likely to evoke the operant. A valuable way to conceptualize reinforcement is by listing the necessary and sufficient conditions, as follows:

- **Behavior** occurs.
- Stimulus **change** during or immediately following response.
- Subsequent **increase** in likelihood of response class on subsequent occasions of exposure to the stimulus.

There are two basic types of reinforcement, namely "added reinforcement" and "subtracted reinforcement."

Added Reinforcement

Added reinforcement (+R) is a behavior change process in which the addition of a stimulus during or immediately following a response, results in an increase in the likelihood of the behavior on subsequent occasions. That is, the behavior → added reinforcer contingency results in a *strengthening* of the evocative stimulus → behavior functional relation. On subsequent occasions of its occurrence, the evocative stimulus is *more* likely to evoke the behavior because of that history of added reinforcement. The necessary and sufficient conditions are:

- **Behavior** occurs.
- Stimulus is **added** during or immediately following response.

- Subsequent **increase** in likelihood of the behavior on subsequent occasions of exposure to the stimulus.

Subtracted Reinforcement

Subtracted reinforcement (–R) is a behavior change process in which the subtraction of a stimulus during or immediately following a response, results in an increase in the likelihood of the behavior on subsequent occasions. That is, the behavior → subtracted reinforcement contingency results in a *strengthening* of the evocative stimulus → behavior functional relation. On subsequent occasions of its occurrence, the evocative stimulus is *more* likely to evoke the operant, because of that previously subtracted stimulus. For example, subtracted reinforcement involves the strengthening of escape behavior. The necessary and sufficient conditions are:

- **Behavior** occurs.
- Ongoing stimulus is **subtracted** during or immediately following response.
- Subsequent **increase** in likelihood of the behavior on subsequent occasions of exposure to the stimulus.

Subtracted reinforcement is unique among the basic principles of behavior in that the consequence is usually a subtracted (reduced or eliminated) version of the evocative stimulus. In a subtracted reinforcement contingency, the evocative stimulus is an aversive stimulus and the behavior functions to reduce or eliminate (i.e., subtract) contact with that stimulus.

Punishment

Punishment (P) is a behavior change process in which a change in stimulation, during or immediately following a response, results in a decrease in the likelihood of the behavior on subsequent occasions. That is, the behavior → punishment contingency results in *suppression* of the evocative stimulus → behavior functional relation. On subsequent occasions of its occurrence, the evocative stimulus is *less* likely to evoke the operant. The consequence suppresses the relation between the evocative stimulus and the behavior. The necessary and sufficient conditions are:

- **Behavior** occurs.
- Stimulus **change** during or immediately following response.
- Subsequent **decrease** in likelihood of the behavior on subsequent occasions of exposure to the stimulus.

Added Punishment

Added punishment (+P) is a behavior change process in which the addition of a stimulus, during or immediately following a response, results in a decrease in the likelihood of the behavior on subsequent occasions. That is, the behavior → added punishment contingency results in *suppression* of the evocative stimulus → behavior functional relation. On subsequent occasions of its occurrence, the evocative stimulus is *less* likely to evoke the operant because of that previously added consequence. The necessary and sufficient conditions are:

- **Behavior** occurs.
- Stimulus is **added** during or immediately following response.
- Subsequent **decrease** in likelihood of the behavior on subsequent occasions of exposure to the stimulus.

Subtracted Punishment

Subtracted Punishment (–P) is a behavior change process in which the subtraction of a stimulus during or immediately following a response, results in a decrease in the likelihood of the behavior on subsequent occasions. That is, the behavior → subtracted punishment contingency results in *suppression* of the evocative stimulus → behavior functional relation. On subsequent occasions of its occurrence, the evocative stimulus is *less* likely to evoke the operant because of that subtracted consequence. The necessary and sufficient conditions are:

- **Behavior** occurs.
- Stimulus is **subtracted** during or immediately following response.
- Subsequent **decrease** in likelihood of the behavior on subsequent occasions of exposure to the stimulus.

Extinction—The Fifth Principle of Behavior

Extinction

Extinction is the fifth basic principle of behavior. It was not included in the table of consequences because it is the absence of a consequence rather than the addition or subtraction of a consequence. However, extinction is no less important a principle and conditioning process than the four other principles.

Operant behaviors are a function of the reinforcer that maintains them. ***Extinction*** (EXT) is a behavior change process in which a behavior maintained by added reinforcement no longer generates the added reinforcer and the behavior subsequently decreases in likelihood.

The word "extinction" can be used to describe a behavior change *process*, a *procedure* of withholding the reinforcer that has maintained a behavior, or the *effect* that it generates—the elimination of the evocative stimulus → behavior functional relation from the subject's repertoire.

Unlike reinforcement or punishment, which involve changes in the postcedent (i.e., after the behavior) environment (i.e., adding or subtracting stimulation), extinction of a behavior that already has a history of reinforcement involves *no* postcedent change in the environment. In other words, nothing of significance is added to, or subtracted from, the environment when the behavior occurs. In extinction, the focus is on the reinforcer *not* occurring; the behavior fails to produce a change in the environment that it generated in the past.

Unlike punishment, the other behavior-elimination process, extinction actually changes the contingency of reinforcement that was maintaining the behavior. It therefore *weakens* the evocative stimulus → behavior contingency rather than merely *suppressing* it through superimposing a punitive contingency over a reinforcing contingency. The necessary and sufficient conditions are:

- Previously reinforced **behavior occurs**.
- **Reinforcer does not occur**.
- Subsequent **decrease** in likelihood of the behavior on subsequent occasions of exposure to the evocative stimulus.

Following instatement of an extinction procedure, the rate of the behavior may initially briefly increase. This spike in the rate of the behavior is called an "***extinction burst.***" There may be a series of extinction bursts during the extinction process, although they will gradually become less frequent and prominent. An extinguished behavior tends to be more readily reconditioned if a reinforcer is reintroduced at some point. This is presumably because some residual structures in the subject's nervous system remain susceptible to the contingency.

As we discuss in detail below, extinction is effective but not usually necessary. An errorless approach arranges the environment so that few to no "errors" (i.e., occurrence of the target behavior) happen to begin with while a replacement behavior is installed. This reduces or eliminates the need to utilize extinction, which is surely unpleasant, although not as unpleasant as punitive procedures.

Once a behavior has become extinct, the subject may occasionally exhibit instances of the behavior when exposed to the appropriate stimulus. This is sometimes unfortunately called "spontaneous recovery," but there is nothing spontaneous about it.

Schedules of Added Reinforcement

Each occurrence of a particular behavior does not always result in added reinforcement. This is the case with behaviors we train such as sitting on cue for a treat as well as behaviors not being trained by others, such as pulling a slot machine arm and money being awarded. A ***schedule of added reinforcement*** sets the rule that determines which responses, among a series of responses, will be or have been reinforced. Let's start with the simple schedules of added reinforcement. We then address some compound schedules.

Continuous reinforcement (CRF) sets the rule that a reinforcer is added after each and every occurrence of the behavior. Continuous reinforcement produces a steady and reliable increase in the rate of responding and is best suited in training through the initial acquisition phase. It also generates two other notable schedule effects. First, behaviors maintained on continuous reinforcement are highly susceptible to extinction. Behavior maintained on continuous reinforcement that is then put on an extinction schedule will tend to extinguish very quickly. Second, behaviors maintained on continuous reinforcement tend to become topographically stereotypical. Variability in the form of a behavior can be useful when you are selecting ones to reinforce and ones not to reinforce when shaping new response class forms.

As well as being a conditioning process and the product of that conditioning, extinction can also refer to the schedule of added reinforcement relevant to that conditioning. An ***extinction*** (EXT) schedule sets the rule that *no* responses within a series of responses will be reinforced. Extinction is the opposite of continuous reinforcement, and predictably, it has the opposite effect on responding. Extinction generates a decrease in responding, the course of that decrease is largely determined by the kind of schedule of added reinforcement the behavior was on before extinction was instated. A behavior previously maintained on continuous reinforcement will tend to extinguish quickly and steadily. A behavior previously maintained on a sparse intermittent schedule of added reinforcement (discussed below) will be less susceptible to extinction and the course of the decrease will be more gradual.

An ***intermittent schedule of reinforcement*** is any of several specific schedules that share the general rule that added reinforcers follow some, but not all, occurrences of the behavior. Behavior on an intermittent schedule is less susceptible to extinction and the form is more variable than behaviors maintained with continuous reinforcement. These schedules include reinforcing after a fixed or variable number of responses, duration the behavior is maintained, or after the first behavior after an interval of time has passed. In variable schedules, one identifies a mean average number of responses or duration but reinforcement it delivered around that mean in a variable and seemingly random manner. Of most importance to us is the variable ratio schedule, because most problematic behaviors are maintained on such a schedule. In addition, differential reinforcement starts with extinction and continuous reinforcement but is then gradually put onto a variable ratio schedule. Therefore, coverage of the variable ratio schedule sets the occasion for our discussion of differential reinforcement and its application.

A ***variable ratio*** (VR) schedule sets the rule that reinforcement will be added following the final response class member after a variable number of response class members around a specific mean average number of response class members has occurred. "Variable" means that reinforcer is delivered in a seemingly random manner around the mean specified in the schedule. It is important to avoid getting too far away from the mean.

The schedule effects associated with the VR schedule are very important for changing behavior. Responding under a VR schedule usually occurs at a high rate. In addition, behaviors on VR schedules are highly resistant to extinction, all the more so the higher the ratio. This can be useful when training a behavior that one wants to be resistant to extinction, but it can be a real problem when trying to extinguish a problem behavior that was on a sparse variable ratio schedule of reinforcement.

Mechanical engineers (utilizing the natural science of behavior and thereby also engaging in behavior engineering) design slot machines to operate on a VR schedule because this schedule maintains the highest rate of responding in relation to the number of reinforcers provided. Unlike the vending machine, the slot machine delivers its reinforcers on a seemingly random schedule, which is in fact a VR schedule. As you would expect, subjects on VR schedules may exhibit the target behavior a vast number of times before a reinforcer is delivered (persistence), assuming the ratio is thinned gradually enough. The ratio of reinforced to unreinforced behaviors can be stretched gradually, but if it is stretched too far and/or too quickly, the ratio may become strained and the behavior can actually extinguish.

Compound schedules of reinforcement are schedules involving two simple schedules such as the ones just covered, put into effect at the same time. The most important among the compound schedules are the differential reinforcement schedules.

Differential reinforcement is a compound procedure in which a response class form or forms are targeted for added reinforcement and other members of that response class are targeted for extinction. Notice that not just any behavior or class of responses is reinforced while some other behavior or class of responses is extinguished. Differential reinforcement describes a procedure that involves targeting a specific response class *form* or response class *forms* for reinforcement and *other members of that same response class* for extinction. Recall that members of the same response class may differ topographically, but they share the same effect on the environment.

Not all procedures that are commonly considered to be differential reinforcement are, in fact, technically, differential reinforcement according to the traditional definition provided. If a particular functional reinforcer (i.e., the reinforcer that has been maintaining the target behavior) is deemed inappropriate for use in a differential reinforcement program, the behavior used to replace the target behavior will be of a different response class, by definition, since a different reinforcer is used. In this case, simply because a different reinforcer is used, the procedure cannot be considered differential reinforcement under the traditional definition. If the functional reinforcer is a subtracted reinforcer and the technologist wishes to avoid using aversive stimulation to support the replacement behavior and so uses an added reinforcer instead, that too would not be a true differential reinforcement procedure. In these cases, the reinforcer maintaining the problem behavior is often problematic because it is harmful in one way or another, or the trainer wishes to avoid using escape from aversive stimulation as a reinforcer because that would mean repeated exposures to aversive stimulation. Commonly, *all* of these procedures are referred to as "differential reinforcement procedures" among animal behavior technologists and animal trainers. However, I adopt the broader view here, that differential reinforcement can include replacement of response class forms *and response classes* to avoid the awkwardness of differentiating between differential reinforcement procedures and "differential reinforcement-like" procedures. However, take note of the distinction between traditional definitions and some contemporary usages of term "differential reinforcement."

There are several variations of differential reinforcement, each of which may be appropriate under different circumstances. These variants are defined by the relation between the target behavior and the extinguished non-criterion behaviors. ***Differential reinforcement of incompatible behavior*** (DRI) is a differential reinforcement procedure in which the reinforcement-targeted response class members or response class form is mutually exclusive with respect to the extinction-targeted response class members. ***Differential reinforcement of alternative behavior*** (DRA) is a differential reinforcement procedure in which the reinforcement-targeted response class members or response class form, while compatible with the extinction-targeted response class members, is a *specific* and *different* response class form or set of response class members. ***Differential reinforcement of other behavior*** (DRO) is a differential reinforcement procedure in which *any* response class member other than the extinction-targeted response class members or response class forms is targeted for reinforcement. There are benefits and detriments associated with each of these procedures and each is more appropriate under different circumstances.

Motivating Operations

There is another kind of antecedent stimulation that impacts upon contingencies and conditioning of operant behaviors called the "motivating operation," which should not be confused with the colloquial term "motivation," which tends to be seen as a mystical force within the so-called (i.e., fictional) "mind." A natural science interpretation of "motivation" would likely involve a situation in which a person thinks about the reinforcer that may be accessed when they think about behaviors that might be evoked to access it. But, though thinking is real behavior, it is private and inaccessible, making it less useful in the training setting. It is more productive to focus on the three-term contingency made up of observable and measurable behaviors and stimulus changes. That being said, the unfortunately named "motivating operation" is actually a stimulus or the process of applying that stimulus.

Biological evolution has resulted in bodies that are structured in such a manner that certain forms of stimulation (called "***unconditioned reinforcers***") may reinforce behaviors that function to generate behavior without any previous conditioning to establish them as reinforcers. Unconditioned reinforcers include such things as air, food, water, and sex. Other stimuli can act as reinforcers but only after being paired with other established reinforcers. ***Pairing*** refers to repeatedly following a neutral stimulus immediately with an established reinforcer, such that the neutral stimulus comes to be effective as a reinforcer as well, at which point, it is called a "***conditioned reinforcer***." Conditioned reinforcers include things like money, compliments, and in dog training, a clicker, or praise.

The effectiveness of conditioned reinforcers is conditional on continued pairing with the established reinforcer. The effectiveness of unconditioned reinforcers is conditional upon motivating conditions within the body that are caused by motivating operations. The unconditioned reinforcer may, depending on the occurrence of motivating operations, be completely ineffective as a reinforcer, be highly effective as a reinforcer, or be somewhere in between. Indeed, the stimulus may even act as an aversive stimulus under certain motivating operations.

Motivating operations (MO) are stimulus events that cause conditions within the body that temporarily alter (a) the effectiveness of a stimulus acting as a reinforcer, and (b) the current likelihood of all behaviors that have been reinforced by that stimulus (Michael, 2007, p. 375). Motivating operations can be a challenging topic to fully appreciate, but the preceding explanation will be made more effective by describing the more common kinds of motivating operations. ***Deprivation*** with respect to an added reinforcer will temporarily make it *more* effective as a reinforcer, making behaviors that access it *more* likely. ***Satiation*** with respect to an added reinforcer will temporarily make it *less* effective as a reinforcer, making behaviors that access it *less* likely. For example, if you are "hungry" (i.e., deprived), then food will be more effective as a reinforcer for behaviors that function to access food. In contrast, if you are "full" (i.e., satiated) with respect to food, then food will be less effective as a reinforcer for behaviors that function to access it. Indeed, if you are well satiated with regard to what would otherwise be a very effective unconditioned reinforcer, it can even become quite aversive. This brings us to the third condition that acts as a motivating operation. If a stimulus is ***aversive*** (i.e., tends to generate escape behaviors), this makes behaviors that function to access it (i.e., approach) less likely and behaviors that function to escape it (e.g., flight or scaring it away) more likely.

In our contingency analysis, the motivating operation is a fourth term and comes before the evocative stimulus thusly:

$$\text{MO} \rightarrow \text{S}^{\text{Ev}} \rightarrow \text{Behavior} \rightarrow \text{Reinforcer}$$

The motivating operation has a temporary effect and so it should not be considered a continuously stable component of contingencies. But, the motivating operations influencing the three-term contingency should be considered where appropriate. For example, training with treats before, rather than after dinner will make for better training because the dog will be deprived rather than satiated and hence the food will be a more effective reinforcer and the behavior more likely to occur when cued. As another example that goes to our rationale for applying DRO, if a stimulus is highly aversive, then escape behaviors will be evoked. But, if these are problematic behaviors that you seek to change, then making that stimulus less aversive will reduce the likelihood of escape behaviors, thereby allowing you to prompt and reinforce an acceptable replacement behavior. Changing the emotional reaction to the stimulus involves changing the motivating conditions under which that problem behavior occurs. This is discussed in a later chapter.

Respondent Conditioning

It is useful to appreciate the conditioning of respondent behaviors because this knowledge will help you understand the potential respondent benefits of the DRO procedure.

Respondents are a class of innate behaviors insensitive to consequences. Respondent contingencies involve a two-term contingency of the stimulus → response form. This is in contrast to the operant three-term contingency of the stimulus → response → stimulus form.

The body is structured such that when the appropriate antecedent stimulus occurs (called the "***eliciting stimulus***" in the case of respondents), a very (species-) specific unconditioned reaction occurs.

The stimulus that elicits this reaction is referred to as an ***unconditioned stimulus*** (US), and the reaction it elicits, an ***unconditioned response*** (UR). In other words, no conditioning is required for that response to occur. Since these relations exist because of biological evolution acting on the genes within a population across generations, they are related to biological imperatives. Examples include salivating in response to food in the mouth and blinking when something touches the eyeball. Unconditioned responses can also include the release of certain chemicals into the bloodstream when an animal is startled.

Respondent conditioning is the process whereby a ***neutral stimulus*** (NS), which does not elicit the behavior in question, comes to elicit a behavior after it has been paired with an unconditioned stimulus (or an established conditioned stimulus). An example of a neutral stimulus is the sound of a clicker before it has been conditioned to elicit a response that functions as reinforcement. The neutral stimulus becomes a ***conditioned stimulus*** (CS) once it elicits the ***conditioned response*** (CR).[3] The conditioned response is usually similar to the unconditioned response. Related to animal training, a piece of food may elicit certain emotional reactions (chemicals released into the bloodstream and certain accompanying neural processes—all respondent) and after pairing the food with a "click" sound, the click comes to also elicit this same emotional reaction. Assuming the conditioned and unconditioned stimuli are at least occasionally paired, the conditioned response will continue to occur. If the conditioned stimulus is presented without the unconditioned stimulus for a number of times, the conditioned stimulus will become neutral again and the conditioned response will not occur (called "respondent extinction"). These processes are illustrated in Figure 2, making it easier to conceptualize.

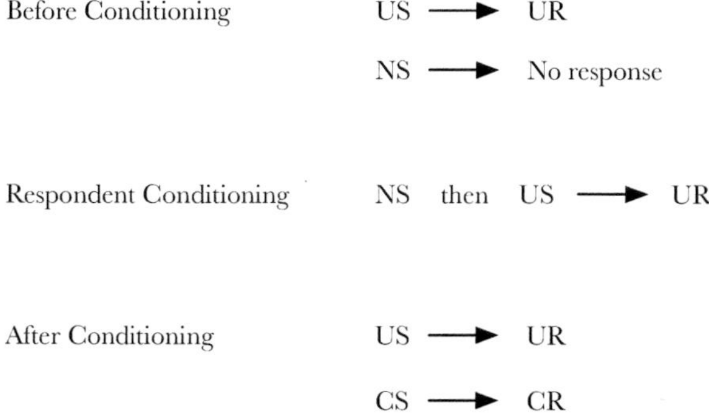

Figure 2. Diagram illustrating the processes of respondent conditioning.

Appreciating the basic respondent conditioning process is important for at least two reasons.

[3] Confusingly, the NS is sometimes called a CS right from the beginning of the conditioning procedure, the idea being that after even the very first pairing, some conditioning has occurred, even if it is not enough for the stimulus to reliably elicit the response.

First, respondent conditioning is how conditioned reinforcers are established and maintained. Pairing a click sound with a treat, for instance, will bring about the elicitation of the same kind of response to the click as occurs to the treat. This appetitive emotional response is respondent and how it was conditioned to occur in reaction to the click is respondent. This appetitive emotional response is maintained by at least occasionally pairing the click with the treat and this too is respondent. The click sound can now function as a reinforcer just as the treat does, but reinforcement is an operant process. The fact that it was achieved with respondent conditioning and involves a respondent emotional reaction does not make its use as a reinforcer respondent in this context. The fact that it is used as a reinforcer does not change the fact that the conditioning to achieve its effectiveness as a reinforcer was not achieved by respondent processes. When used as a reinforcer and described in that context, the reaction it elicits is emotional and respondent, but its role, as a reinforcer, is operant—that is, it follows an operant and increases the rate or relative frequency of that operant on subsequent occasions.

Second, emotional responses are respondents, involving the secretion of various chemicals into the bloodstream and certain accompanying neural processes. We refer to the neural awareness-related after-effect behaviors, of this emotional arousal, as "feelings." Words such as "fear," "panic," "anxiety," "happiness," "anger," "joy," and so on, are simply the labels applied to describe feelings.

Emotional arousal can influence operant contingencies by temporarily restructuring parts of the nervous system to make the body more or less reactive to certain stimuli in evoking operant behaviors, or to make certain reinforcers and punishers more effective. Emotional arousal can render operant behaviors exhibited during that aroused state more energetic in many cases.

However, take note that these are covert (i.e., private) behaviors, and while including them in our analysis can contribute to a fuller appreciation and accounting of behavior, in practical cases, it is usually best to externalize the contingency, relying on stimuli and reactions that can be observed and verified by others. Externalizing a contingency works like this. Let's say that some stimulus elicits an emotional behavior and also evokes an operant or that some stimulus elicits an emotional behavior and then while the subject is aroused, some other stimulus evokes a behavior that it might not otherwise evoke. We might be tempted to identify the emotional behavior or the arousal it creates as the *cause* of the behavior. This intervening (i.e., in between) term might look like this: S^{Ev} → emotional behavior → operant behavior → consequence; or it might even look like this: emotional behavior → operant behavior → consequence. The problem is that the emotional behavior, as a cause of the operant behavior of concern, is private and inaccessible to our observation and manipulation. To ***externalize a contingency***, we trace back through the chain of causes of the operant behavior in question to a point external to the subject that we can observe, measure, and manipulate. In this case, we trace back past the emotional behavior that one might think "causes" the operant to the external stimulus that caused it. Let's say that a stranger elicited the emotional behavior (which is respondent), and also flight (which is operant). Rather than identify the emotional behavior as the cause of the flight behavior, we identify the stranger as the cause. The contingency then looks like this: stranger → flight → escape$^{(-R)}$. Thus, we maintain our focus on the problem operant and on the external and manipulable evocative stimulus, without getting bogged down with any of various intervening private variables. The emotional behavior is not ignored. It is a part of the mediation of the operant behavior, that is, how it occurs biologically. By identifying this contingency as maintained by subtracted reinforcement, we know that aversive emotional behaviors and unpleasant "feelings" may be involved, but again, the focus in maintained on the most productive components of the contingency.

Chapter 2. "Empowerment"

What is Empowerment?

The term *empowerment* came out of a management practice movement in the 1980s. Since then, it has been used within the communities of self-help psychology, motivational training, organizational psychology, and mediation processes, but it has not garnered much serious attention from natural scientists.

There have also been different emphases on empowerment and hence different types of empowerment. Individual, psychological, community, political, cultural, organizational, and other forms of empowerment have been proposed. Here, I use the general term "empowerment" to refer to the behavior of individuals, with an emphasis on processes applicable to both human and non-human animals.

Empowerment can refer to an array of related conditioning processes and effects or outcomes. Careful reading of the literature on the topic suggests that empowerment refers, most fundamentally, to the process of promoting more "power and control" over one's circumstances (e.g., adaptability, capability), and being empowered refers to exhibiting or exercising this power and control (Prilleltensky, Nelson, & Peison, 2001). Prilleltensky and colleagues (2001) use the phrase "mastering the environment," which seems appropriate in a behaviorological sense. In behaviorology, the term "mastery" refers to the highest degree of competence or proficiency in a contingency or set of related contingencies, determined by specific criteria in specific instances. Empowerment might further be thought of in terms of options and choices. Furthermore, this process is commonly said to engender confidence, promote optimism, promote an internal "locus of control" and increase "self-efficacy."

The concept of empowerment, as evidenced by references to feelings or options and choices, is steeped in mysticism, which is likely why it finds a sympathetic discipline in psychology. In any natural science, including behaviorology, natural events are assumed to be fully caused. There is no so called "free will" and hence there is no "choice" in the sense of a free-willing agent initiatively or spontaneously choosing/selecting one option or course of action over another. Certainly, feelings or and beliefs in the notion of free will are common but these are feelings and beliefs—behaviors—and these feelings and beliefs are fully caused as well. Choice and free will *seem* to occur, but that is an illusion caused by our failure to exhibit awareness of all of the causes of our behaviors back through the endless chain of causes. We exhibit a private verbal behavior regarding the selection of one course of action over another, but that selecting behavior is fully caused and that cause was caused and so on. Our failure to recognize all of the causes often results in the occurrence of a belief behavior that we may spontaneously initiate actions.

You may have noticed I refer to the occurrence of behaviors and to people exhibiting behaviors and this may have seemed odd. It seems odd because English (and presumably most or all other languages) are conditioned within a very mystically-oriented verbal community. Behavior happens. It is a reaction. It is not spontaneous and it is not chosen as if independent of the laws of nature. To proceed with a study of behavior allowing for agentialism and the possibility of free will is to abandon the principles of natural science, the only approach to knowledge acquisition that is highly effective.

To be clear, if empowerment is to be considered scientifically, it cannot implicate free will or the presence of a behavior initiating "mind" or to any other non-natural, mystical force, event, or thing. It must refer to actual behaviors, stimuli, contingencies, processes, etc. This must be the starting point, otherwise it is best left to psychology.

Therefore, as we discuss the concepts of "power," "control," "choice," and "options," we must be speaking about behavior-controlling verbal behaviors (including the covert/private verbal behaviors that we refer to as "thinking" and might characterize as beliefs, feelings etc.) These beliefs are real behaviors and they exert real influence over other private verbal behaviors and more overt behaviors, as well as components of contingencies. There is a way to move forward in exploring the notion of empowerment scientifically.

Let us start with a number of concepts and theories that are related to empowerment. Many of these notions are from psychology, so once we introduce them, they may or may not provide much value to a natural science approach to the issue.

Locus of control is a "social learning" theory developed by Julian B. Rotter in 1954. It refers to an individual's belief regarding the source or cause of what happens to them. An external locus of control refers to the belief that what happens to an individual is caused by something external to them (which ultimately is the case), whereas an internal locus of control refers to the belief that what happens is caused by the individual's own choices and actions (perhaps proximally in many cases, before the chain of causes extends out into the rest of the environment on the other side of the skin). Regardless of the actual causes of behavior, the notion of locus of control can be framed in terms of real belief behaviors.

Self-efficacy is a "social cognitive" theory developed by Albert Bandura (Bandura, 1977). It is broadly defined as "the belief that one is capable of performing in a certain manner to attain certain goals. It is a belief that one has the capabilities to execute the courses of actions required to manage prospective situations. Unlike efficacy, which is the power to produce an effect (in essence, competence), self-efficacy is the belief (whether or not accurate) that one has the power to produce that effect" (Wikipedia.org, 2009). Bandura proposed that when self-efficacy is high, the individual is more inclined to take up challenges. As with locus of control, if we stick to the proposition that a belief occurs regarding the effectiveness of the individual exhibiting that belief to contact reinforcers, the concept can be informative.

Learned optimism is a psychology term coined by Martin Seligman (Seligman, 1990/1998). Seligman developed the related concept of learned helplessness, which we discuss further below. Learned optimism, which is the opposite of pessimism, represents the behaviors of attributing obstructed access to reinforcers as external rather than internal or personal (similar to locus of control), variable rather than static and permanent, and specific to the situation. Seligman proposed that one could be conditioned to behave in ways that would evoke the term "optimistic" rather than "pessimistic" and "helpless," and that the result would be greater "self-actualization" and "happiness." As with the other concepts discussed, the idea relates to private verbal behaviors.

What these related concepts all have in common is that they relate to private verbal behaviors that might evoke the word "belief" or "assumption." Private verbal behaviors are real behaviors, but they are observable only to an audience of one—the person exhibiting the behavior. As such, these notions are of limited practical value. These ideas do however, illuminate the contingencies related to the concept of empowerment. While many of the concepts relate to private verbal behaviors of the belief and attribution form, empowerment can encompass the kinds of overt contingencies that someone is under that involve both the covert and overt behaviors. While the psychological perspective on empowerment is likely to emphasize "mental transformation" and "cognitive" forces, a behaviorological perspective would emphasize real and more overt contingencies (i.e., the overt behaviors and the externalized stimuli that evoke and consequate them). This is not to say that behaviorological interventions cannot include "talk counseling."

Whatever empowerment is, it would result in the evocation of verbal evaluations of one's capability to exert control over the environment. It would be the result of fluency in the behaviors under consideration and the contacting of reinforcers. I proceed under the following definition: ***Empowerment*** *involves the various conditioning processes that result in effective and efficient access to added reinforcers and/or escape from subtracted reinforcers as well as those outcomes and the relevant contingencies under which they occur.* The result of this actual fluency would result in private verbal behaviors that reflect this mastery. In other words, a high level of fluency such as 100% for instance may result in a series of belief behaviors that do not involve any aversive emotional reactions that are generated by extinction. In other words, if behaviors occur every time the evocative stimulus occurs, this would be the result of an effective conditioning process and effective reinforcement, the result of which would be certain appetitive emotional reactions and concomitant private verbal behaviors related to the subject's "ability" to access reinforcers." The emphasis is placed on the effective conditioning of behaviors and the verbal evaluational behaviors are considered secondary. To be empowered is to be adaptable and capable of operating on one's environment, and secondarily, to be aware of this in a way that promotes further adaptive responding.

It quickly becomes apparent that whatever is meant by "empowerment," it is generally a beneficial state of affairs for an organism, resulting in greater levels of personal satisfaction, as vague as that is. It also involves a kind of feedback loop in that an empowered individual is more likely to engage in behaviors that will support being empowered. Individuals said to be disempowered would likewise tend to find themselves without an effective repertoire and avoiding contingencies that might otherwise lead to the expansion of their repertoire of effective responding. Our consideration of the topic of conditioning for empowerment sets the occasion for identifying training practices that will support the expansion of adaptive repertoires and rehabilitating the behavioral repertoires of those who tend not to exhibit them. Thus, the topic begins to reveal an importance worth exploring.

In more behaviorological terms, empowerment comes down to contingency and the availability of escape from aversive stimulation. If consequences are contingent upon the behaviors of an individual and effective escape behaviors are readily available, effective repertoires can be shaped and maladaptive contingencies become displaced. If consequences tend not to be contingent upon the behaviors of an individual, or escape behaviors are not readily available, adaptive repertoires are unlikely to be conditioned and indeed there are well-known side-effects related to noncontingent or inescapable aversive stimulation, consideration of which will inform our understanding of empowerment and disempowerment.

This brings us to the concept of obstructed access to reinforcers (be they added or subtracted). If life always went well and there never were any obstructions to accessing reinforcers, there would be no such thing as empowerment or disempowerment because the distinction would be empty. Implicit in the notion of empowerment is obstruction or challenge that requires a means of overcoming it—accessing a reinforcer requires responding.

Individuals need a way to deal with inevitable extinction trials (leading to frustration) or aversive contingencies in a way that promotes fluency and hence the elicitation of appetitive emotional reactions. Although a repertoire of effective reinforcer-contacting behaviors is required, what might be of more importance is a repertoire of behaviors effective in responding to aversive contingencies, particularly to those involving extinction and noncontingent or inescapable aversive stimulation. Mastering general behavioral tactics (some might call them "coping skills") under such contingencies that function to overcome the challenge as opposed to failing to do so and experiencing the aversive side-effects of such contingencies is what empowerment versus disempowerment seems to reflect. In other words, life does not always "go our way," despite our efforts to access certain reinforcers, and we may respond either with a lack of "power and control," with depression or disruptive emotional reactions, or we may engage the circumstances in ways that either eventually access the reinforcer or we can try to find other sources of reinforcement with minimal frustration. Which of these tendencies is conditioned will depend, of course, on the history of conditioning that the individual has experienced. However, before we move on to identify empowering tactics, let us explore disempowerment further.

What is Disempowerment?

Disempowerment is the opposite of empowerment—it is a lack of effective and adaptive or productive behaviors patterns. Disempowerment includes familiar behavioral phenomena variously known as behavioral suppression, disruption, interference, conditioned helplessness, and response depression.

Disempowerment is often framed in terms of "prediction and control"—whether an individual effectively predicts and controls what happens to them. This is usually considered with regard to aversive stimulation, but lack of prediction and control of appetitive stimulation can also generate problematic behavior patterns (Job, 2002). Prediction and control, in behaviorology, is related most closely to *contingency*, the dependent or functional relations between a behavior and its controlling variables. If a consequence is contingent upon the occurrence of a behavior, then we recognize and confirm the functional relation between them and the degree of consistency or correlation between them in that regard is often referred to as the *degree of contingency*. The words "prediction" and "control" are colloquial rather than technical. Predicting is a behavior and might refer to the verbal behavior of expressing (exhibiting) a belief in the likelihood of something. It might also refer to the degree of contingency being referred to in that verbal behavior. People often muse "what are the odds?" but the odds of something that happens occurring is 100%. Everything that happens is the only thing that could have happened. Odds and probability reflect our ignorance regarding the relations involved and our ignorant prediction of whether that thing will happen or not.

Control is also related to contingency. A "sense" of control refers to private verbal behaviors that relate to the effectiveness of the subject's behavior in accessing added reinforcers or escaping subtracted reinforcers. It might also refer to the actual level of effectiveness in such contingencies.

As we proceed through discussion of prediction and control, we refer to the degree of contingency that allows for effective responding. A high degree of contingency, particularly as it relates to aversive contingencies, allows for effective avoidance behaviors, and if need be, effective escape behaviors where these options are available. A failure to avoid or escape aversive stimulation can reflect a low degree of contingency, that is, an inconsistent relation between a behavior and the consequences it generates. In other words, escape behaviors are not always successful. It can also reflect contingencies in which neither avoidance nor escape are possible. The effects of a low degree of contingency that results in inconsistency and/or impossible-to-escape aversive stimulation is key to "prediction and control" as these terms are used in this context. If one can readily avoid or escape aversive stimulation consistently, predictability and control are said to be present and if one cannot, they are said to be absent and the presence or absence of this has important ramifications for subsequent behavior (aversive emotional behaviors and other side effects, including conditioned helplessness).

The term *depression* is used in psychology, usually as a general term to refer to Major Depressive Disorder, but it is a vague term in this context and often refers in part to reports of feelings. Behaviorologically, depression refers to a broad or specific reduction in responding. Response depression can result from a generally low level of experienced reinforcement or from a low degree of contingency, particularly as it relates to aversive stimulation, as discussed above. Response depression is evident in the behavioral phenomenon referred to as conditioned helplessness, which I will discuss in detail below.[4] The research on these topics can inform us in conditioning tactics for empowerment and for identifying and rehabilitating disempowered individuals. Response depression is just one of the effects of lack of control and prediction of aversers and reinforcers (Job, 2002). Below, I outline others for a more complete coverage.

Effects of Uncontrollable and Unpredictable Aversive and Appetitive Stimulation

Job (2002) called attention to the fact that lack of control and prediction of appetitive stimulation can generate similar (though not identical) problematic behavioral effects to lack of control and predictability of aversive stimulation.

---

[4] This process is more commonly known as "*learned helplessness*." The word *learn* is colloquial and is generally avoided in behaviorology in favor of the technical term "*condition*" in order to express the passive rather than active/agential/initiative nature of the process. I frame the concept as "*conditioned helplessness*" to avoid the colloquial word and its agential implication.

After reviewing the literature, Job identified the following effects of lack of control and prediction of aversive stimulation:

- impaired shock escape;
- impaired operant conditioning;
- impaired discrimination conditioning;
- dissociation of speed and conditioning effects;
- impaired frustration escape;
- reduced activity;
- effect survives long delay;
- immunization effect;
- analgesia;
- body weight loss;
- finickiness;
- prophylaxis by prediction;
- EUUE (effects of uncontrollable/unpredictable events) removed by glucose [meaning administration of glucose minimizes the effect]; and
- increased fear.

Job (2002) found similar effects in studies of lack of control and predictability of appetitive stimulation, minus reduced activity, increased fear, and removal of the effects by glucose. These three effects are "fear"-related and, without aversive stimulation, fear is not generated.[5] What is most interesting is that many of the problematic effects we commonly associate with uncontrollable and unpredictable aversive stimulation also occur when the subject cannot control or predict appetitive stimulation. In a very broad sense, predictability and controllability are empowering, and lack of these capabilities is disempowering. Establishing clear response-contingent consequences is key to promoting empowerment.

Of most interest to us is a cluster of these effects having to do with response depression (i.e., impaired shock escape, impaired operant conditioning, impaired discrimination conditioning, dissociation of speed and conditioning effects, impaired frustration escape, reduced activity, analgesia, and perhaps increased fear.) We also discuss "safety signaling" as indicated above by "prophylaxis of prediction."

Response Depression and Conditioned Helplessness

Response Depression

As mentioned, the term "depression" is colloquial. It is commonly evoked to label (or sometimes ineffectively to describe, or fallaciously to explain) an episodic or chronic syndrome of unpleasant feelings of "sadness." This is, of course, a private experience that is not readily subject to scientific verification by others, limiting its usefulness in a technology of behavior. A psychological approach might medicalize the term, label it as a "syndrome," classify it as "abnormal" or maladaptive and apply standardized and general treatment solutions, usually including talk therapy and medication.

---

[5] Note that the word "fear" is often used by psychologists (including behavior analysts) to refer to an amalgam of respondent emotional behaviors and operants, but this is a rather colloquial usage. Emotional behaviors involve the release of chemicals by glands into the bloodstream. After-effect awareness-related behaviors, if they occur, are referred to as "feelings." Feelings may subsequently be tacted in various ways, one of which is "fear." So, the word "fear" refers to a verbal behavior, describing a feeling that is generated by emotional behaviors.

A behaviorological analysis would involve externalizing the contingencies to emphasize the more verifiable overt behaviors, their rate or relative frequency and their functional relationship with the environment.

The traditional behavioral approach, sometimes called the Lewinsohnian behavioral approach, explains response depression primarily as a low rate of response-contingent added reinforcement, with the emotional arousal and unpleasant experience being byproducts (Ferster, 1973; Kanter et al., 2008). Others have suggested that this alone is insufficient as an explanation and posit that escape and avoidance repertoires contribute to response depression just as prominently as a lack of response-contingent added reinforcement. Response depression, according to this view, is the product of both a lack of appetitive contingencies *and* an abundance of aversive contingencies (Kanter et al., 2008). Kanter and colleagues (2008) succinctly describe response depression as:

> (a) losses of, reductions in, or persistently insufficient levels of positive reinforcement as per Lewinsohn (1974), and (b) increases in environmental aversive control (negative reinforcing and punishment contingencies). When chronic, both processes may be seen as functioning as enduring motivating operations for depression (Dougher & Hackbert, 2000).

More current behavioral views recognize the emotional arousal elicited by reduced contact with response-contingent added reinforcers. Although many instances of response depression may be accounted for by the description above, rule-governed avoidance repertoires (self-talk rules and directives of a depressive nature), at least in humans, likely play a prominent role in maintaining depression (Dougher & Hackbert, 2000; Kanter et al., 2008). Since our emphasis is on species who exhibit relatively simple verbal behaviors, we do not explore rule-governed behavior.[6]

---

[6] This is not to say that non-human animals are unaffected at least to some degree by rule-governed behavior and other private verbal operants. A preponderance of the evidence suggests at least some capability in that regard.

Response depression can be defined and operationalized as a reduction in general activity, disruption of conditioning, and/or a failure to exhibit escape behaviors or a failure to persist during extinction. This concept does require further fleshing out to be most useful since reduction in activity and disruption of conditioning can be challenging to measure in applied settings. As outlined above, our emphasis is on problematic forms of response depression, resulting from minimal response-contingent added reinforcers and/or abundant aversive contingencies. The depressed responding then results in less contact with response-contingent reinforcers. It is also worth noting that certain operants occurring during response depression, that might contribute to a failure to respond effectively, can be reinforced as well. In other words, "moping," "ruminating," or other operant behaviors occurring during response depression can be reinforced.

We are not concerned with reduced responding resulting from more powerful competing contingencies, such as when we carry out differential reinforcement, or in distraction situations (Nation & Woods, 1980). Our concern is with the more problematic instances of response depression—those that result in contact with fewer reinforcers and reduce general behavioral wellbeing.

Depressed responding is a major problem; it is incompatible with empowerment and general behavioral well-being. If we cease exhibiting behaviors that may contact reinforcers, we do not contact as many reinforcers and hence our general well-being deteriorates.

Conditioned Helplessness

Seligman, Overmier, and their colleagues, throughout a number of works discussed here, proposed that conditioned helplessness was the basis for response depression. Response depression is a broader concept than conditioned helplessness, a concept well known among animal trainers and behavior technologists (Overmier, 2002). The notion of conditioned helplessness, pre-dated by the phrase "fear from a sense of helplessness"

(Mowrer & Viek, 1948), denotes not only a specific response depression effect (i.e., failure to exhibit escape behaviors) but also a hypothesized mechanism (i.e., response–consequence independence).

In experiments, reminiscent in their outrageous brutality of Harlow's work with monkeys, Seligman and coworkers (Overmier & Seligman, 1967; Seligman & Maier, 1967) performed horrific experiments on dogs to expand their repertoire regarding fear conditioning.[7] They arranged experiments that would explore the "interference phenomenon" associated with inescapable aversive stimulation. Demonstrating the *helplessness effect,* they strung some dogs up in a harness that prevented them from escaping and affixed electrodes to their feet. In numerous trials, they presented a tone, followed by an intense electric shock. Some dogs in other groups were allowed to exhibit a behavior that allowed them to turn off the shock. The dogs that could continue with the experiments and were not dead or otherwise incapable of continuing due to the shocks were put, 24 hours later, into a shuttle box—a crate or box with two sides and a barrier in the middle that could be jumped over. The experimenters sounded the tone, followed by intense shocking of the floor on the dog's side of the box. The dogs in each group initially responded similarly: barking, yelping, howling, running frantically about, defecating and urinating until they scrambled over the barrier. If the dog managed to get over the barrier and into the other side of the box after the tone but before the shock, they avoided the shock, and if they jumped over after the shock started, they escaped the shock. If they failed to escape the shock, the shock eventually stopped. Dogs that had not previously been exposed to inescapable shocks often succeeded in escaping or avoiding the shock.

Groups of dogs that were previously exposed to inescapable shocks responded quite differently. Although they may have initially responded with extreme agitation, they generally failed to escape or avoid the shock. Through repeated trials, they came to actually remain silent and stop moving around—their

[7] I simply cannot avoid a personal response to these studies here in the body of the book since I will be benefiting from them here. It's a mad world indeed where "learning" more about some phenomenon (such as what happens when you deprive an infant of their mother or expose animals to inescapable intense electric shocks) is considered adequate justification for causing extreme and persistent pain and suffering. A mad and infuriating world indeed!

responding had been depressed. Seligman and colleagues proposed the quite obvious, "helplessness," as the reason for this depressed responding.

Follow-up experiments included increasing the strength of the shock to see if stronger stimulation would cause the dogs to escape—it did not. The experimenters also chemically paralyzed some dogs to see if all the ineffective wiggling in the harness might have somehow affected the results—it did not.

They also tested groups with 24, 48, 72, and 144 hours between the initial treatment and the escape test. Overmier and Seligman (1967) found that the depression effect dissipated through time. Seligman and Maier (1967), on the other hand, found that the response depression or helplessness effect did persist, and other researchers have subsequently also found the effect to persist. Later research on rats had much the same results, except that the depression effect did not dissipate over time, even after only a single trial of inescapable shock (Seligman, Rosellini, & Kozak, 1975).

Seligman, Maier, and Geer (1968) also summarize the equally brutal and sickening research of Richter (1957). In these studies, rats were put into water. Those who were repeatedly taken out and put back in persisted in swimming to avoid drowning (swimming—and indeed persistence itself—was likely reinforced superstitiously), as did rats who were allowed to repeatedly escape. These rats (beings who we have every reason to believe experience pain and suffering) swam for approximately 60 hours before drowning. Rats who were not repeatedly removed and put back or allowed to escape gave up relatively quickly and drowned. One might say that when there is no "reason to believe" one can successfully escape aversive stimulation, response depression (and various maladaptive behaviors) results.

In experiments where inescapable, escapable, and control groups of rats were exposed to a different escape task, Rosellini and Seligman (1975) found that conditioned helplessness effects transfer (generalize) to tasks other than the ones where the conditioned helplessness effects were conditioned. This indicates, not surprisingly, that conditioned helplessness or response depression likely affect other activities for the animal and other domains of their lives outside of the specific conditioning arrangement that generated the response depression.

Remember that conditioned helplessness is not only the procedural stipulation of inescapable aversive stimulation, but a hypothesized effect—namely "helplessness." The problem, as it stands, is that helplessness is somewhat vague. However, conditioned helplessness can be understood consistent with basic principles of behavior as the side-effects associated with extinction of subtractively reinforced behaviors. Extinction, as most people are familiar with it, involves failing to additively reinforce a previously additively reinforced behavior and the subsequent decline in the rate or relative frequency of the access behavior. However, there is no reason that extinction must only apply to additively reinforced behaviors. Escape behavior (i.e., behavior maintained by subtracted reinforcement) can also be extinguished, a process Fraley (2008) referred to as *reequilibration*.[8] In the case of extinguishing escape behaviors, escape behaviors that may have been subtractively reinforced in the past (not necessarily in the setting in which it is currently being applied) are no longer reinforced, meaning, escape is no longer allowed, and the rate or relative frequency of the behavior would decrease. The side-effects would be typical of extinction but would likely generate more intense aversive emotional arousal since it involves a failure to escape an aversive stimulus rather than a failure to access an added reinforcer. The "helplessness" effect that Seligman proposed is more parsimoniously consistent with the well-established natural science principles of behavior explained by the side-effects associated with extinction of subtractively reinforced behaviors.

In the end, the picture we are left with is that, when faced with inescapable aversive stimulation, an initial flurry of escape responding occurs, but if this is not quickly successful, a depression in responding takes place. That is, escape

---

[8] The word reequilebration is used because in all cases, the rate or relative frequency of the behavior returns to preconditioning levels—it *re*turns to *equilibrium*. Extinction can be applied to additively and subtractively reinforced behaviors as well as additively and subtractively punished behaviors and in the case of extinguishing punished behaviors, the rate or relative frequency increases rather than decreases, making "extinction" a problematic word since it is usually evoked by a decrease in something. See Fraley (2008) for more in-depth coverage of this topic.

behaviors are extinguished, resulting in a brief increase in the rate and intensity and variability of responding, followed by a decrease in the response class and eventually full extinction (i.e., response depression). It also seems that previous escape conditioning resulted in less depressed responding in the shuttle box tests. Seligman and colleagues proposed that the individual comes to be conditioned such that the aversive stimulation is response independent and this promotes a kind of helplessness (recall that behavior is driven by a history of reinforcement). Other hypotheses have been proposed to explain these effects, but it is beyond the scope of this book to explore them in detail (see Levis, 1976).

Again, the key feature here is exposure to inescapable aversive stimulation. Life involves exposure to various aversive events on a regular basis. Just how aversive the stimulation must be to generate conditioned helplessness, how much exposure to inescapable aversive stimulation is required, how unsuccessful the subject must be in escaping it, and how persistent is the depression effect, probably varies. For individuals who develop a history of being unsuccessful in escaping aversive stimulation, some degree of response depression and other problematic effects can be expected. Some individuals are exposed to more aversive events than others, and some are more successful than others in escaping the events. Some may have experienced a conditioning history that immunizes them to some degree against the response depression effects (i.e., they had previous successful escape conditioning). It seems likely that response depression or conditioned helplessness is a matter of degree rather than an all-or-none effect. It may occur in reaction to even mild aversers, depending on the individual's history of conditioning and genetic influences. Individuals who have problems with aversive emotional responses (which might be termed "fear, anxiety or panic"), for instance, tend to experience response depression to some degree.

In exploring how to prevent or rehabilitate such conditioning, it is wise for professionals to be observant for response depression and indeed other problematic effects of aversive stimulation. Obviously, promoting independent, confident, and resilient responding is important, both proactively and reactively, and can improve an animal's general behavioral well-being.

Chapter 3. Training to Promote Empowerment

Introduction

Thus far, I have provided a primer in the basic principles of behavior to provide a foundation for appreciating the behavioral effects of certain contingencies and how to arrange contingencies (training) to promote empowerment. I have also provided a brief summary of some of the relevant theories and concepts related to empowerment.

In this chapter, I bring together much of what we have covered into a set of general tactics that may be used proactively to promote the greatest empowerment possible. This involves utilizing an errorless approach to training in general and training subjects to exhibit a few general patterns of behavior, that might be characterizes as "good general coping skills."

In the final chapter, I address the rehabilitation of subjects already disempowered in some manner and to some degree.

Basic Strategy and Tactics for Promoting Empowerment

Below is a set of practices that, together, can help prevent disempowerment problems and arm the subject with a repertoire of behaviors and patterns of behaving that will promote empowerment.

Tactics for Conditioning Empowerment

The following set of tactics should be considered when training anyone. They are geared to empowering individuals and inoculating them against disempowerment.

- Ensure that the subject's physical needs are met, including medical care, adequate nutrition, exercise, play, and other forms of stimulation that act as motivating operations for operant behaviors.

- Ensure a high General Level of Reinforcement (GLR). This means accessing more, and more effective, reinforcers in general.

- Generally, maximize *response-contingent* added reinforcement, particularly in the early stages. This means ensuring that the subject's behavior (rather than the whim of others, or mere chance) generates consistent consequences.

- Ensure that an errorless approach is used in any training or contingency management planning, particularly early in the training, arranging the environment to make the desired behavior likely to occur and then reinforcing it so that problematic behaviors never or rarely need to be extinguished.

- Proactively avoid aversive stimulation, particularly in early stages. Where contact with aversers cannot be avoided, utilize an errorless differential reinforcement of other behaviors (DRO) procedure to desensitize the subject to the averser(s) when possible. Condition quick and effective escape behaviors.

- Implement persistence training to (see the section below on training persistence):

    - Identify and train effective coping behaviors;

- implement continuous reinforcement in the acquisition stage;
- implement a gradually thinning intermittent variable schedule of reinforcement after the acquisition stage; and
- adjust schedules and other training tactics as required to maintain the coping behavior.

- Implement industriousness training (see the section below on training industriousness):
  - Set industriousness-related criteria in training and differentially reinforce industrious behaving; and
  - recognize unplanned instances of industriousness and reinforce them.
- Implement creativity training activities (see the section below on training creativity):
  - Perform free-shaping games and training projects;
  - incorporate novel responding (creativity) criteria in training projects;
  - when appropriate in later stages of training, allow for alternative operant behaviors (response generalization) to contact reinforcement rather than just a specific response; and
  - recognize and additively reinforce unplanned instances of creativity.

Strategy for Conditioning Empowerment

Conditioning empowerment involves establishing a history of reinforcement for adaptive behaviors. Importantly, this involves two important phases or components, both of which are necessary. They are as follows:

- First, an errorless approach is utilized in order to condition a tendency to exhibit reinforcement-contacting behaviors.

- Second, minor frustrations are introduced while conditioning general behavioral tendencies supportive of responding adaptively/constructively to working through or around obstructed access to reinforcers (i.e., extinction) and aversive stimulation.

In other words, first, the subject is conditioned to exhibit what some might refer to as "confidence" so that they will readily exhibit behaviors to access reinforcers without inhibition or suppression. Second, because life inevitably involves minor frustrations and aversive stimulation from time to time and we also want the subject to be able to "handle" this well, minor frustrations are introduced in an incremental manner, while effective/adaptive patterns of behavior (i.e., "behavioral tendencies") are conditioned and the subject comes to "cope" with such events.

These patterns of behavior ensure the greatest likelihood of the subject accessing added reinforcers and avoiding the frustration and other problematic effects of obstructed access to reinforcers or aversers. One might say that these patterns of behavior will prepare the subject with the general problem-solving skills needed to access the greatest possible enjoyment in life.

A pattern of behavior is another way of referring to a set of response classes or response class forms that share some feature or criterion. We can identify common elements across responses that we can then characterize based on a principle with which they are consistent. For instance, a well-established characterization of a pattern of behavior within behaviorology is *discrimination*. A subject does not discriminate (Moore, 2008).

Discrimination is not a behavior. However, if across responses, a principle or common element, such as in this case, a decrease in the range of evocative stimulus features controlling a response class, then this principle can be identified and the pattern of responding characterized in accordance with it. The patterns of behavior that I discuss below might be thought of as *tendencies*, or more agentially *strategies*, because they reflect a characterization of set of responses that share some feature, and in this case, these features tend to reflect a general and commonly effective behavioral approach (i.e., "coping skills" or "problem-solving skills") for accessing reinforcers.

The patterns of behavior that we aim to condition include persistence/industriousness, creativity, and resilience. To the degree that a subject is conditioned to exhibit these general patterns of responding, the subject will be less likely to experience frustration and response depression and they will be more likely to experience "satisfaction," leading to what we might call empowerment and behavioral well-being.

These behavior patterns are conditioned in the same way as any more specific behavior—by generating instances of the behaviors and reinforcing them. Behavior objectives are established and the environment is manipulated in order to generate the contingencies of reinforcement that increase the likelihood of the target patterns of behavior on subsequent occasions. The subject is set up for success, criteria for reinforcement are established that will be achievable, clear, and consistent, and the criteria are changed incrementally, thereby shaping persistent, creative, and resilient responding. Research has demonstrated various ways of achieving success in promoting these behavior patterns and avoiding response depression and frustration, and the tactics described here are based on that research.

In more colloquial terms, we prove to the subject that that they can operate effectively on their environment, even when they face common everyday challenges or even uncommon frustrations. They are armed with the most effective repertoires of behavior for doing so. This means allowing them more controllability and predictability over their environment and preparing them for the adverse conditions that are common and unavoidable in everyday life.

But first, the errorless approach is foundational for all of this training and it is discussed in detail before proceeding.

Errorless Training

The last 100 years have seen a dramatic paradigm shift within the behaviorological orientation with respect to how problematic behaviors are explained and resolved. In this section, I describe the early eliminative and trial-and-error approaches to changing behavior, some key developments since then that have resulted in a shift toward a more constructional approach, and the errorless training paradigm that represents best practice today.

Thorndike's Trial-and-Error Approach

In 1898, E. L. Thorndike conducted seminal experiments on non-human animals designed to elucidate their "intelligence." Thorndike summarized the method of his experiments in this way:

> I chose for my general method… merely to put animals when hungry in enclosures from which they could escape by some simple act, such as pulling at a loop of cord, pressing a lever, or stepping on a platform. … [F]ood was left outside in sight, and his actions observed. Besides recording his general behavior, special notice was taken of how he succeeded in doing the necessary act (in case he did succeed), and a record was kept of the time that he was in the box before performing the successful pull, or clawing, or bite. This was repeated until the animal had formed a perfect association between the sense-impression of the interior of that box and the impulse leading to the successful movement. When the association was thus perfect, the time taken to escape was, of course, practically constant and very short.

This experiment was an early and quintessential example of the trial-and-error approach to conditioning, what Thorndike referred to as "accidental success."

It can still be said that the subject's repertoire was shaped via selection by consequences. Ineffective behaviors were extinguished, and, assuming effective behaviors eventually occurred, they were reinforced. This is not now, nor was it then, seen as the only way to train/teach someone to exhibit a behavior, but it was popular as a means of explaining the behavior of non-human animals in particular.

There are two major problems with the trial-and-error paradigm as applied to training animals (be they non-human or human). First, trial-and-error training is highly inefficient. The number of potential non-criterion behaviors that would occur prior to the criterion behavior being stumbled upon can be very high. In some cases, the criterion behavior may never occur. With so many potential non-criterion behaviors, the criterion behavior becomes rather unlikely. The subject is trained "what *not* to do," but as we sometimes colloquially say, there is an almost infinite number of behaviors not to "do" when only one response class form meets the reinforcement criterion. Second, a great many non-criterion behaviors (i.e., "errors") are exhibited in trial-and-error training, leading to a great many extinction trials, surely resulting in frustration and other well-known side-effects associated with aversive stimulation, including aggressive behaviors and response depression (see Sidman, 2001).

A More Robust Perspective on Shaping

Since Thorndike presented his research and the trial-and-error approach became a popular explanation for the evolution of repertoires of behavior and an approach to changing behavior, a number of important events have accumulated, causing a shift away from this paradigm. Below, I describe a few of the key events.

Individual response class forms and repertoires of behavior can be shaped in the way Thorndike described and many behaviors are shaped through a trial-and-error process. However, Skinner (1953, pp. 91–106) recognized another manner of shaping behavior that could be used when teaching/training others. As opposed to merely selecting for (i.e., reinforcing) criterion behaviors in their final form and selecting against (i.e., extinguishing), non-criterion behaviors in their final form, Skinner described the shaping of response class forms by differentially reinforcing successive approximations of the criterion behavior. In other words, Skinner proposed identifying an incipient response class form, one that already occurs quite readily, and reinforcing it, making it more likely and hence making an even closer approximation occur more readily as well. The approximations are then reinforced in an incremental manner until the criterion (or terminal) response class form occurs. Rather than extinguishing all final-form responses except the criterion response class form, which may or may not occur at all, let alone quickly, Skinner described how one may begin reinforcing right from the beginning.

Prompts and Other Antecedent Control

Importantly, Skinner (1968) discussed the importance of prompts and other antecedent manipulations in generating target behaviors in general (pp. 222–223). Skinner (1953, p. 213) wrote of "supplementary stimulation," including prompts as a means of raising the probability of a response class. Thorndike's approach provided the *opportunity* for the behavior to occur, but otherwise did not manipulate the environment in ways that made the criterion behavior *more likely* than other behaviors until after it occurred and could be reinforced. Skinner's approach to shaping in the broadest sense and teaching/training more specifically allowed for arranging the environment in ways that made the criterion behavior more likely and hence other behaviors less likely.

This can be achieved through prompts—stimuli other than the intended primary evocative stimulus that contribute to generating the criterion behavior so that the to-be evocative stimulus may take on greater stimulus control as the behavior is reinforced in its presence. Preclusion of alternatives is another method of generating the criterion behavior.

Indeed, any antecedent manipulation that increases the likelihood of the criterion behavior or an approximation of it, is useful in the shaping of specific response class forms and repertoires of behavior in general.

Terrace's Errorless Discrimination Procedure

Another major milestone in that shift occurred when Terrace (1963) devised and tested an errorless procedure for discrimination training. This procedure well illustrates the difference between trial-and-error and errorless approaches to training. Here, I use an example of traditional discrimination training (referred to as "evocation training" by many behaviorologists) that corresponds to Terrace's experimental arrangement. In traditional discrimination training, a chicken is placed in an experimental chamber in which a keypad is installed on the wall.[9, 10] When the keypad is illuminated red, pecking the keypad is additively reinforced with food and when the keypad is illuminated green, pecking the key is extinguished. Through repeated trials, responding stabilizes with a high rate of responding in the presence of the red illuminated key (the evocative stimulus, or, S^{Ev}), and no responding in the presence of the green illuminated key (the extinction stimulus, S-Delta, or S^{Δ}). The extinction curve under such contingencies tends to be moderate, meaning that quite a few extinction trials occur before responding stabilizes.

Terrace introduced a set of procedures called "errorless discrimination" that reduced or eliminated the unnecessary extinction trials. First, the chickens were placed in the experimental chamber and the keypad was always illuminated red and pecking the red illuminated key was additively reinforced on a variable interval schedule (though a continuous schedule could be used as well, particularly at first during the acquisition phase). Second, once

[9] See Ferster and Skinner (1957, chapter 3) for a detailed elaboration of the experimental chamber.

[10] Please note that I do not condone experimentation on non-human animals that requires any kind of exploitation, which includes keeping them in captivity, regardless of whether the experiment causes physical or behavioral harm as well and regardless of how "valuable" anyone believes the results to be. Non-human animals cannot provide informed consent. As a rule of thumb, if an experiment and everything that conducting it requires would not be acceptably carried out on young children (with or without parental consent), then it would be no more acceptable to carry it out on a non-human.

conditioning had been achieved (i.e., responding to the S^{Ev} was stable), the S^{Δ} was introduced in a fading in procedure along intensity (i.e., brightness), duration, and wavelength (i.e., color) dimensions. The green illumination started off brief and dark so as to draw less attention. Gradually, the dimensions of the green key illumination were manipulated until they were equal to that of the red key. What Terrace found was that chickens trained using the traditional discrimination procedure exhibited vastly greater number of "errors" compared to those training with the errorless discrimination procure. The only chickens in the experiments that exhibited "emotional" responses in the presence of the S^{Δ} were those trained under the more traditional approach, which allowed for vast numbers of extinction trials.

Goldiamond's Constructional Orientation

In 1974, Israel Goldiamond wrote an extensive and seminal paper, calling into question the pathology orientation that was common at the time. The pathology orientation views problematic behaviors as abnormal, leading to an emphasis on the eliminating or "curing" of such behaviors. The pathology orientation married well with the medical model of categorically labeling problematic behaviors, usually by topographic features. The pathology orientation tended to support an eliminative approach to resolving these problematic behaviors. Behavior reduction procedures, such as punishment and extinction, along with problematic antecedent control procedures, such as severe deprivation, were common and the behavioral approach to changing behavior, what was then called "behavior modification," came to be seen as unethical and even illegal in some cases.

Goldiamond, proposed a change from the pathology orientation to what he called a constructional orientation. The ***constructional orientation*** emphasized the *building* of more adaptive repertoires as opposed to the *eradication* of repertoires via the eliminative approach. The emphasis was placed on added reinforcement and new, more adaptive, behaviors that would displace the problematic behaviors. In doing so, Goldiamond set the stage for the behavior replacement model and the idea of displacing problematic behaviors with more acceptable behaviors, which allowed for an emphasis on added reinforcement-based procedures.

Though the constructional orientation does not rule out eliminative procedures, this paradigm shift further supported the general strategic approach of resolving problematic behaviors with as little need for aversive stimulation as possible.

Shifting Paradigms and the Shaping of the Errorless Approach

The landmark contributions to science by Skinner in the area of the shaping of response class forms and repertoires of behavior and the utilization of prompts and other antecedent control measures, by Goldiamond in the area of constructional over pathological orientations to behavior, and by Terrace in the area of errorless discrimination training led to the more general approach to training that we now call "errorless training."

It was within the above described cultural milieu that the ***errorless training*** approach was shaped. In applied settings, behaviorologists, behavior analysts, and behavior technologists began to view problematic behaviors as normal reactions to specific sets of contingencies and that changes in the behavior could be achieved by arranging new contingencies that would support more adaptive behaviors that would displace the problematic behavior. Repertoire building with added reinforcement came to replace aversive behavior reduction procedures. The emphasis on arranging the antecedent environment in such a way that makes the problematic behavior (i.e., "errors") unlikely, while establishing a strong history of reinforcement for less problematic and more adaptive behavior is becoming the best practice standard.

Application of the Errorless Approach

The target behavior to be trained may be involved in a behavioral excess or a behavioral deficit. In a behavioral deficit case (as can be the case when training a new behavior outside of the problem environment, so that it may later be applied to that environment to displace a problem behavior) is a behavior that the subject currently does not engage in or engages in but not in reaction to the target evocative stimulus. In these cases, non-criterion behaviors would comprise all response classes and response class forms that the training environment might otherwise evoke. In behavioral excess cases, the non-criterion response class or response class form is the target problem behavior to be eliminated. Under a behavior replacement model, the target problem behavior is tracked and its reduction is a significant part of the behavior objective, but the replacement behavior is also trained and tracked.

In all such cases, the technologist plans how to manipulate motivating operations, other function-altering stimuli, and evocative stimuli requirements, which can be faded in the maintenance phase.

Errorless training can be applied in a wide variety of circumstances and under various training objectives. In many cases, non-criterion behaviors can be rendered impossible or highly unlikely while simultaneously the criterion behavior can be made highly likely. Under some circumstances, fewer of these tactics may be available and errors can occur. Extinction of non-criterion behaviors is still consistent with the errorless approach but extinction trials are minimized to the greatest extent possible.

Let us explore a number of ways in which the environment may be manipulated in order to promote the criterion behavior over non-criterion behaviors. The technologist may eliminate evocative stimuli for non-criterion behaviors where possible.

They may also gradually introduce problematic antecedent stimuli with a fading in procedure after the criterion behavior has been strengthened with a history of reinforcement outside of that environment. This is a part of the errorless approach discussed below. The idea is that the problematic stimulus is introduced at a minimal intensity along any of various dimensions so as to exert minimal control over the subject's behavior, allowing criterion behaviors to be prompted and reinforced. The stimulus intensity is then increased gradually along any of several dimensions until the criterion behavior has been installed.

The technologist may also utilize motivating operations, abolishing for non-criterion (target) behaviors and establishing for the criterion (replacement) behavior.

The technologist may instate all of the tactics above as appropriate, in order to generate the criterion behavior. At first, criterion behaviors are maintained on a continuous reinforcement schedule, until they have stabilized, at which point one may transition to a suitable intermittent schedule (e.g., as a variable ratio schedule).

The Errorless Approach

The ***errorless approach*** may be summarized as follows: (a) manipulate the environment such that the criterion behavior is as likely to occur as possible and non-criterion behaviors are unlikely to occur; and (b) establish a strong history of reinforcement for the criterion behavior until it displaces the non-criterion behavior.

A ***graded approach*** (sometimes called a "***prompt and fade***" or "***fading in***" approach) refers to (a) breaking projects down into smaller more manageable steps or subprojects that can be worked separately and in an appropriate order, and (b) breaking problematic stimuli into component parts and/or arranging exposure along dimensions such as distance, duration, orientation, animation, presence of other distracting stimuli, etc., in a graded manner from least provocative to most, and at a pace that allows for installing replacement behaviors.

The graded approach might be thought of as a means of achieving errorless conditioning and hence may be thought of as being encompassed by the term "errorless approach." The errorless approach is a powerful paradigm in changing behavior and this strategy underlies good contingency management planning.

The errorless approach represents training behaviors in the most productive and supportive manner possible. However, an errorless approach to conditioning can only be the beginning. If we are not conditioned to effectively face challenges and frustrations head on, then we are more likely to "fall to pieces" so to speak, when we do face such contingencies. Eventually, we do need conditioning with regard to life's inevitable frustrations and challenges. This inoculates us against frustration, depression, and helplessness.

General Patterns of Behavior that Contribute to Promoting Empowerment

Now that we have covered how to avoid errors and frustration, which is particularly helpful at the beginning of training, we cover how to supportively introduce minor frustrations and condition effective problem solving and coping behavior patterns. Let me be clear. I am not condoning the use of aversive methods and tools in training new behaviors or for resolving problem behaviors! What is being covered here is different. What is being described here is training subjects to respond to minor everyday aversive contingencies that cannot be always avoided. Let's face it, life does not always provide us with errorless opportunities—if there were no "errors," there would be no such concept as "errorless." If we are not conditioned to work around frustrations, we will "fall to pieces," when faced with such contingencies.

In the following sections, I elaborate on the concepts of persistence/industriousness, resilience, and creativity as putatively important features of achieving empowerment, that "sense" of "power and control." These patterns of responding are not empowerment per se, but they are general behavioral tendencies that can contribute to establishing a set of circumstances that might evoke the word "empowerment." These are not necessarily the only behavioral tendencies involved in contributing to empowerment either, but they will serve as a core starting point.

If life always went well and there never were any obstructions to accessing reinforcement, there would be no such thing as empowerment or disempowerment. Implicit in the notion of empowerment is obstruction or challenge that requires a means of overcoming it. Individuals need a way to deal with inevitable extinction trials (leading to frustration) or aversive contingencies (leading to fear) in the real world without giving up or emotionally "falling to pieces." We need behavioral tactics for minimizing the likelihood of obstructed access to reinforcers or aversive contingencies, but also tools for dealing with inevitable everyday instances of it. Sometimes, it is just time to go inside when you'd rather play outside. To summarize, life does not always go our way, despite our efforts to access certain reinforcers, and we can respond either with a lack of "power and control," with response depression or disruptive emotional arousal, or by persisting and, with creativity, finding a way to access the reinforcer or some other reinforcer instead.

I address the broad, general strategy of arranging for greater likelihood of productive and adaptive problem-solving behaviors for helping to achieve the best possible general behavioral well-being. For these purposes, empowerment is conditioned by conditioning the following patterns of behavior:

- persistence/industriousness ("stick-to-it-ness," effort, "keep trying"/"try harder");
- creativity (novel, productive variation in contacting reinforcers); and
- resilience (emotional stability and "bounce back" rather than disruptive emotionality).

These behavior patterns allow us to operationalize concepts such as confidence, control, power, optimism, locus of control, and self-efficacy, while making them more accessible and measurable without reference to private verbal behaviors or presumed intervening variables. The three behavior patterns listed above are interrelated. For example, training persistence and creativity tends to produce resilience, and each benefits the effectiveness of the other.

The processes that generate these behavior patterns encompass the various conditioning processes that we arrange for in empowerment training. We can train these behavior patterns in the same way that we train other, more specific, behaviors. A number of practices can enhance persistence/industriousness, creativity, and resilience, and we can also avoid conditioning that would be detrimental to them. Strategically, the subject is set up for success when the environment is arranged such that the subject is persistent, creative, and resilient, and these behavior patterns are reinforced, as the level of difficulty is gradually increasing (i.e., an errorless approach).

We do not know what the animal is thinking in terms of "confidence" and where they attribute their locus of control (etc.), but we can determine whether they persist and use novel, productive behavior, and that conditioning is not inhibited or disrupted by emotional arousal.

Although I am loath to write it, if it helps the reader appreciate the goal, the animal comes to "believe" that the world is more or less a stable and consistent place and, when problems arise, they have the "power" to effectively get what they "want." If they do not succeed at first, they can try again and they will likely eventually be successful. If they are not successful, that is okay because other reinforcers are readily available and extinction is not that big of a deal.

Persistence/Industriousness

Persistence and industriousness are colloquial terms, more or less easily appreciated by all audiences. Since they are closely related, I address them together. Industriousness refers to effort; one who works hard and diligently is said to exhibit industrious behavior. Persistence refers to perseverance of the rate or relative frequency of a behavior once an extinction schedule is instated. In an extinction procedure, the extinction effect is a decrease in responding (i.e., the extinction curve on a graph). When we refer to persistence, we are talking about a long extinction curve rather than a sharp decline—the behavior persists.

Persistence is generally undesirable when the behavior of concern is a problematic behavior (e.g., growling when someone approaches a dog while they play with a toy), but is usually desirable when the behavior of concern is acceptable or helpful (e.g., sitting rather than running all over us while we get ready to go outside). We typically want problem behaviors to extinguish quickly and want installed desirable behaviors to persist, even when we cannot readily reinforce each instance of their performance.

With that introduction, both persistence and industriousness are addressed in turn, but note that they are closely related principles.

Persistence

Behavioral momentum is defined by an aggregate response measurement of the rate of the behavior and its persistence during changes in environmental conditions or contingencies (e.g., extinction, shifts to noncontingent reinforcement, or other changes in schedules of reinforcement) (Nevin, Mandell, & Atak, 1983; Plaud & Gaither, 1996). Persistence is therefore a component of behavioral momentum. Since we are specifically interested in the persistence of behavior during extinction, our emphasis is focused on this narrower meaning of persistence. Nation and colleagues (1979) defined persistence as follows: "Persistence refers to the capacity of any learned behavior or effect to survive protracted non-reinforcement (extinction)."

Conditioning for persistence is necessary, particularly for replacement behaviors in contingency management projects, because if the replacement behavior cannot be sustained in the real world outside of the training setting, the project is unlikely to succeed and disempowerment can result (for the guardian as well as the companion animal). Persistence can be an important part of behavioral well-being (how adaptive the subject's behavior is), and adaptive behaviors must be conditioned to persist. Persistence is particularly useful when shaping complex behaviors, which is a useful technique for promoting creativity, as discussed below. One of the most reliable ways of promoting persistence (or behavioral momentum in general), is by manipulating the schedules of reinforcement for the behavior of concern and exploiting the *partial reinforcement extinction effect* (PREE). PREE refers to the tendency of behavior to resist extinction when it is maintained on an intermittent schedule of added reinforcement rather than a continuous schedule of reinforcement (Nation & Woods, 1980; Chance, 2009, pp. 187–188).

It is preferable to start training a new behavior using a continuous reinforcement schedule. The high degree of contingency between the behavior and the reinforcer and the high density of added reinforcers promote quick and effective conditioning. Although a continuous schedule is ideally suited to the acquisition stage of training, behaviors maintained on continuous reinforcement are particularly susceptible to extinction. As soon as the behavior is stable and reliable, it is time to shift to an intermittent schedule. Avoid delaying the transition to the intermittent schedule. As is discussed in more detail below, judiciously arranged failure to access reinforcers generates behavioral variability and also persistence. Nation and Massad (1978) put it this way:

> What may be the more important ingredient in formulating a treatment for clinical depression is not success per se, but failure in the context of success. As dissonant as it seems, the present findings implicate failure as a necessary component for any therapy program that attempts to teach and sustain nondepressive behaviors.

Industriousness

Industriousness refers to effort; one who works hard and diligently is said to exhibit industrious behavior. Industriousness is different from persistence in that it relates to a "try harder" rule rather than a "keep trying" rule, though they are integrally related. Industrious patterns of behavior can be reinforced and also generalized. One who puts in the necessary effort and persists is more likely to contact the reinforcers involved. Industrious behavior is reinforced by establishing criteria for reinforcement in training programs that include effort as a key component. This is explored further in the final chapter, along with ways to promote persistence.

Creativity

Creativity, and the related notion of problem solving, are key aspects of empowerment. Problem solving is the general term referring to contacting reinforcers that are not readily accessible; it is about overcoming frustration. Creativity is useful in problem solving because it helps us find *other* means of accessing the reinforcer. Creativity can be thought of broadly as the occurrence of novel yet worthwhile, effective, and productive behaviors (Fraley, 2008, pp. 786 & 805).

Novel, in this context, refers to behaviors that have not generally been observed following the current antecedent conditions. Novel behaviors that have no utility fail to generate reinforcement and would be generally considered "weird" or "crazy," whereas novel behaviors with utility are creative (Fraley, 2008, p. 786). Glover & Gary (1976) operationalized Torrance's (1966, 1971, discussed in Glover & Gary, 1976) four characteristics of creativity in their set of experiments as:

- fluency (exhibiting a large number of responses);
- flexibility (exhibiting a large variety in responses);
- elaboration, development, and embellishment (building on the responses in terms of productivity); and
- originality (exhibiting productive responses in a nonobvious or statistically infrequent way).

The important point is to operationalize creativity in whatever way works best in the circumstances of the case at hand and track the behaviors quantitatively. You can define creativity more generally by novel responding, or you can break it down into specific measures, such as those used by Glover and Gary, above.

As you can see, creativity is related to persistence and resilience, in that it refers to the subject's general response to challenges or frustrations. Each of the variables I propose here to represent empowerment refers to the quality or quantity of the target behaviors or other interfering behaviors associated with situations. Creativity refers to a quality of responding. Persistence refers to the quantity of responding. Resilience refers to the quantity of interfering behaviors.

Creativity involves novel responding, not with just any behavior but with effective and novel behaviors (Chance, 2009, p. 262). The animal accesses previously inaccessible reinforcers, reduces the response effort, or increases the magnitude of the accessed reinforcer. Consider someone you find very creative. They think "outside the box" and are more likely to find productive solutions, even when those solutions are not evident. They also tend to persist and they are resilient; they have to be—otherwise they would have given up before finding a creative solution. Consider also the old notion of the fine line between "genius" and "insanity." What is likely being observed here is a high rate of very novel problem solving, some of which turns out to be productive (creative, "genius") and some not productive ("weird," "crazy," or "insane").

A related concept is resurgence. Resurgence is the occurrence of previously reinforced behaviors during extinction trials. Trainers often colloquially say that the animal begins exhibiting every behavior in their repertoire when extinction is instated. Exhibiting behaviors in the current context that proved productive in other contexts might also be thought of as creative, and this can be a basis for promoting creativity.

Creativity, itself, can be conditioned. Conditioning creativity is straightforward: reinforce creative responding rather than merely specified responses (Chance, 2009, p. 264; Glover & Gary, 1976; Pryor, Haag, & O'Reilly, 1969). To promote problem solving in creative ways, set up training sessions in which there is a manageable challenge, and reinforce only novel attempts to access the reinforcer. Instead of allowing only very specific responses, where feasible, allow any operant that achieves the desired outcome for response generalization and novel responses for creativity. Judgment is required here. Set the criteria such that excessive frustration is avoided! As with many of the training tasks in this phase, if training is poorly executed, the subject will become frustrated and disempowered, the opposite of the intended goal. Experience and judgment in setting criteria and managing failures are vital.

Glover and Gary (1976) used an "unusual uses game." Although their game was designed for humans (a species that tends to exhibit particularly complex verbal behaviors, including those which are rule-governed), the basic idea of the game can be adapted to species that exhibit less complex verbal behaviors. It involves setting up a game session with reinforcers available for the following criteria:

- number of responses;
- number of different kinds of responses;
- number of different operants; or
- number of statistically infrequent responses.

Pryor and colleagues (1969) conducted some fascinating research demonstrating not only that creativity can be conditioned, but also how it can be conditioned. They trained two porpoises to exhibit "an unprecedented range of behaviors" by reinforcing only actions that had not been reinforced previously.

Goetz and Baer (1973) conducted similar experiments using human children and novel block-building forms. Using social reinforcers, they found that if they reinforced "new form" construction, new form construction increased, whereas if they reinforced "same form" construction, new form construction decreased. This indicates that if you want to promote creativity, avoid reinforcement for "same old" responding and instead provide reinforcement for novel responding.

Remember that there can be a fine line between confusion and stimulation of creativity. You want to approach that line but not cross it. Especially in the early stages of a rehabilitation project, maintain stability and consistency. Gradually introduce creativity-training at such a pace that lack of predictability does not lead to response depression. Set the subject up for success even when you are setting them up for failure!

Resilience

Resilience relates to the extent to which other behaviors interfere in current contingencies. The interference is usually the result of aversive emotional arousal that sets the occasion for these interfering operant behaviors. The extent of the interference usually depends on how aversive the emotional responding is and how quickly the subject can recover from it or work through or around it. Note that interference behaviors can be adaptive, usually by redirecting the subject's attention away from aversive stimuli, but resilience is about not requiring this redirection. Resilience, then, refers to minimizing excessively emotional behaviors and quickly recovering from excessive emotionality by working through it, resulting in fewer interfering behaviors.

Resilience can be a challenging notion to analyze because emotional arousal is not readily observable and measurable under normal training circumstances. We commonly observe operants and some readily observable reflexes as an indication of respondent processes, but this also leaves us studying the phenomenon indirectly. In behaviorology, we typically circumvent reference to emotional responses in operant contingencies because of this difficulty (and maintain adherence to scientific principles). We can do so without ignoring the importance of emotional arousal. A stimulus elicits the emotional arousal, which then sets the occasion for the operants. We can "cut out the middleman" (so to speak) and identify just the evocative stimulus and the resulting observable operant. Operant escape behaviors imply aversive stimulation and so aversion is implied. This is called "externalizing the contingency." We do not claim that the emotional responses do not exist or even that they are unimportant, but rather we trace back in the sequence from the readily quantifiable operant, past the intervening emotional arousal, to the external environmental event that caused them both because it can be more readily analyzed scientifically. These events occur in a causal chain, and so we study the functional relationship between the independent variable (i.e., the stimulus) and the dependent variable (i.e., the behavior) in a manner that can be directly observed and measured, without relying on presumed intervening variables, implied or not.

Resilience refers to responding with minimal emotionality in the face of aversion/frustration and "bounce-back," as many animal trainers put it. Bounce-back commonly refers to a quick return to a stable rate or relative frequency of responding without exceeding the elasticity of what is being stretched. In other words, bounce-back describes the tendency of an animal to return to pre-sensitization responding after startling or becoming influenced by emotional arousal (e.g., experiencing an adrenalized response). We assume this to correspond to the dissipation of disruptive emotional arousal. Some individuals bounce back quickly, whereas others become and remain emotional (i.e., behavior is disrupted) for an extended time.

Bounce-back is a common tendency included in many "temperament tests" (especially dog temperament tests). In these tests, a loud noise is usually generated behind the dog, and a measure is made of how long it takes the dog to return to "calmness." It is thought by some that a dog with quick bounce-back is more "stable" in various ways than a dog with slow bounce-back. Certainly, we know that excessive emotionality ("falling to pieces" they might say) can be detrimental to health and that excessive physiological emotional arousal can interfere with conditioning.

A resilient subject might be said to be one who does not respond with excessive emotionality, or who returns to pre-sensitization rates of responding quickly after they have been sensitized. This seems an important feature of empowerment, which should not be ignored just because it involves emotional arousal.

Subjects can be immunized against excessive emotionality. Subjects who never experience obstructed access to reinforcers (i.e., frustration) become emotional easily when exposed to extinction trials. In my other job as a Krav Maga instructor, we train in hand-to-hand combat under high levels of stress generated by exhaustion and the fear of being hurt or failing to perform well. We also engage in rather hard combat sparring. By engaging in these kinds of training activities, which include stress and being hit, when faced with a truly violent situation in the "real world," we experience less intense of an adrenal response and perform better. This is a form of stress immunization as well, and follows the same general approach that we are exploring here.

Constant *inescapable* frustration or aversive stimulation can also lead to excessive emotionality and response depression, in some cases. The key to conditioning for resilience is to set the subject up to experience *manageable* frustrations, which are not excessive for their conditioning history, and condition them to overcome the frustration (perhaps, most usefully, with persistently creative responding). Another approach is to promote persistence and creativity, which will provide the "tools" the subject needs in order to overcome frustrations. Minor frustrations and aversive experiences that the subject can work through can "demonstrate (i.e., prove) to them" (in a manner of speaking) that these aversers are manageable and hence "no big deal."

Chapter 4. Rehabilitating Disempowerment and Related Problems

In this final chapter, I build on what has been covered thus far and provide guidance on rehabilitating subjects who are under the various contingencies represented by the term "disempowerment." The strategies, tactics, and procedures in this chapter are not a one-true-way proprietary system. Nor are they my own personal invention. The content is shaped by research and theoretical analysis in the behaviorological literature.

Disempowerment and Other Conditioning Circumstances

Disempowerment is not a "diagnosis." Neither is "response depression." Neither of these terms define response classes and the contingencies of which they are components. At best, they are vague and ambiguous characterizations. In behaviorology, diagnoses are functional and based on the formal contingency analysis. They identify the functional reinforcer maintaining a real response class or set of response class forms and the manner of contact with that reinforcer. For example, *SME: Aversive Social Interaction* is a functional diagnosis identifying *escape* (E) as the function, *socially mediated* (SM) as the manner of contact and *aversive social interaction* as the more specific (but still general) kind of stimulus. Disempowerment and response depression do not qualify. It is important to be clear that a number of behavioral phenomena might be operative in circumstances that evoke the terms "disempowerment," "response depression, "conditioned helplessness," etc. In such cases, the specific behaviors and their controlling relations need to be identified and addressed directly.

As the research on conditioned helplessness has shown, response depression often resulting from extinction of subtractively reinforced escape behavior and the resulting side-effects, or "fallout," if you will, that occur.

Terms such as "disempowerment," "response depression," "general risk aversion," and "conditioned helplessness" verbally economic, though colloquial, call attention to these clusters of circumstances/contingencies. This is why I have entertained the terms, as least in as much as they call attention to the issue and makes proper analysis more likely.

What the contents of this chapter *do* provide is some general strategies and more specific tactics to address specific problems involving subjects who are experiencing indications of having undergone such histories of conditioning and are now exhibiting their side-effects.

A subject may demonstrate some or all of the characteristics of what we are calling "disempowerment," and may do so to varying degrees. Disempowerment can be a useful construct insofar as it points to specific behavioral deficits that are likely to impact on the subject's well-being. We exhibit the term "disempowerment" when there is an indication of response depression, lacking "confidence," and/or excessively narrowed or "safe" behaving, as opposed to flexible and creative behaving, the result of which is reduced access to added reinforcers and a general reduction in the subject's behavioral well-being. The subject may seem generally risk-averse and seem to lack "confidence." They may not experiment much, or, if their behavior is usual in this regard, they may "fall apart" in the face of extinction and frustration, failing to try again or failing to try something different.

In most cases, technologists (or behaviorologists) will be under contingencies to resolve a specific problem behavior of some kind, typically a problem involving emotional arousal, such as those commonly labeled "separation anxiety/panic," "fears," or other "anxieties." My books *Resolving Fears, Phobias, and Anxieties: An Errorless Differential Reinforcement Approach for Professionals* and *Resolving Fears, Phobias, and Anxieties: A Guide for Dog Guardians* were written specifically for such problems. If a technologist observes what might be such indications of restricted or maladaptive patterns of behavior, further probing in the functional interview process should focus on elaborating the specific conditioning processes and patterns of behavior involved. If it is deemed suitable, the technologist might include resolution strategies in the contingency management plan for helping to resolve or alleviate disempowerment issues. They might find that it is best addressed after the primary problem is resolved, especially in minor cases, or that some tactics can begin and continue throughout and after the primary contingency management plan. Or they might find, particularly in severe cases, that it requires immediate intervention and that addressing it may, in full or in part, help alleviate the primary problem they were called on to help resolve. It is in this context that I provide the contents of this chapter.

General Guidelines for Rehabilitating Disempowerment

Colloquially and agentially, rehabilitating disempowerment and response depression involves gradually demonstrating to the subject that they can indeed effectively operate on their environment. Their history of conditioning has involved more or less inescapable aversive stimulation (or even simply response-independent added reinforcement during very confusing training projects), which has generated response depression and/or rigid behaving. The strategy is simply to establish a history of conditioning characterized by highly response-contingent added reinforcement, to reinforce industriousness, persistence, and creativity, and address specific aversive contingencies. Instances of appropriate operant behavior should be reinforced with a high degree of contingency on a continuous reinforcement schedule at first, while instances of creativity, industriousness/persistence, and resilience should be recognized and reinforced throughout.

The guidelines provided below are general in nature. They must be adapted to the particulars of the problematic responding being observed and analyzed.

The general approach to rehabilitation might include from among these options:

- Preclude aversive contingencies.
- Satisfy general needs and adjunctive measures.
- Increase General Level of Reinforcement (GLR).
- Ensure response-contingent reinforcement.
- Consider instating from among these interventions:
    - Errorless differential added reinforcement of other behaviors (DRO) (See O'Heare 2018a, 2018b); or
    - Seligman's rehabilitation procedure.
- Instate as appropriate training for:
    - persistence/industriousness;
    - creativity; and/or
    - resilience.

I provide a brief description of each guideline and follow those with detailed elaboration of those guidelines that require the more extensive coverage.

Preclude Aversive Contingencies

The first thing to do is identify and eliminate, one way or another, any aversive contingencies that the subject is currently under. Often, these contingencies can be discontinued or contact with the evocative stimulus precluded. This may require a bit of creativity in some cases. Sometimes, this is not feasible, and in those cases, the subject needs to be trained quick and easy avoidance, or if need be, escape behaviors, or better, the emotional reaction to the aversive stimulus is changed. Changing emotional reactions is carried out via respondent extinction or respondent counterconditioning. Counterconditioning is the least aversive option, which can be achieved with an errorless differential reinforcement of other behaviors (errorless DRO) procedure (see O'Heare, 2018a, 2018b). But in any event, begin any intervention by eliminating the sources of the problem.

Satisfy General Needs and Adjunctive Measures

At the same time that aversive contingencies are being identified and eliminated, the technologist should inquire about general lifestyle issues and routines. Evaluate exercise, nutrition, varied appetitive stimulation, medical issues, and care, etc. Recommend improvements as appropriate and legal. In many cases, reinforcement impoverished environments can generate disempowerment-related issues. This calls for a gradual increase in moderate aerobic exercise and after a period of a high degree of consistency/routine, varied reinforcing stimulation (i.e., enrichment). It also means increasing the general level of reinforcement, the topic discussed next.

Increase General Level of Reinforcement

"General level of reinforcement" (GLR) refers to "the number, strength, and duration of reinforcers per unit of time" (Cautella, 1994, cited in Ledoux, 2014, p. 378) GLR involves the quality and quantity of added reinforcers that the subject accesses on a regular basis (see Ledoux, 2014, pp. 377–380, for a summary of GLR and its relation to response depression). A reduction in, or simply a low level of, GLR can result in response depression. A vicious cycle ensues because the response-depressed individual becomes less likely, because of less responding, to access added reinforcers. Whether a subject operates in a reinforcement impoverished environment to begin with, the intervention instated to resolve problematic behaviors involved a general reduction in the subject's contact with added reinforcers, or even if there is

simply room to increase the general level of added reinforcement in a subject's life, efforts to generally increase the subject's contact with added reinforcers can have a beneficial effect on the subject's physiological condition and quality of emotional arousal they operate under. By increasing the subject's GLR, the occasion is set to reduce escape and avoidance behaviors and instead engage in more reinforcement-accessing behaviors.

Increasing the GLR for a subject is not necessarily a complicated matter. It can simply involve identifying effective activity reinforcers (i.e., Premack principle-related behaviors) and planning ways to incorporate these activities into the dog's everyday life. This might involve non-social activities such as an increase in the number of and quality of toys to which the dog has access. It may also involve a number of social activities, such as social play, walks, outings to special places like dog parks, or to go swimming, or just for a car ride. The key is to identify activities that are actually effectively reinforcing of behavior for the individual dog rather than being something that one might assume ought to be reinforcing. These activities should be made contingent upon specific desirable behaviors.

Ensure Response-contingent Reinforcement

Throughout the intervention, an emphasis should be placed on ensuring that consequences are never arbitrary or response-independent. Ensure that consequences, both in intervention procedures and in everyday life, are consistent and response-dependent. Operant behavior is behavior that is said to operate on the environment. It is vital that the subject's behavior generates the events that happen to the subject. That said, the household should not be run like a boot camp! The behaviors need not involve a high degree of response effort. Desirable behaviors may simply be reinforced when they occur. The key here is consistency.

Consider Errorless Differential Reinforcement of Other Behaviors (Errorless DRO) or Seligman's Rehabilitation Procedure

Some subjects may become disempowered due to previous conditioning experiences that are no longer operative, while others involve ongoing contact with aversive stimulation. Subjects can be trained to escape directly (e.g., flee), either with differential subtracted reinforcement or errorless differential added reinforcement procedures (see *Aggressive Behavior in Dogs*, 2nd edition or later). This does not require a change in the emotional reaction to the stimulus, but it does reduce contact with the aversive stimulus and is suitable in many cases.

Changing emotional reactions is another way to resolve problems involving aversive contingencies and is likely preferable in cases relevant to disempowerment. This might involve cases of aggressive behaviors (socially mediated escape) or perhaps more often as it relates to disempowerment, it might involve flight behaviors (direct escape) that might evoke the label "fear." In such cases, a procedure that changes emotional behaviors is useful.

Changing emotional behaviors directly might involve a number of respondent extinction procedures (e.g., exposure and response prevention or flooding), but these are quite drastic and aversive procedures that are best avoided where possible. The other major conditioning process that changes emotional behavior is respondent counterconditioning, which, in practice, is achieved with a procedure known as "systematic desensitization."

However, in most cases, the emphasis is placed on the operant target behaviors and replacement behaviors, as well as the conditioning processes to achieve those changes. Under the operant paradigm, one excellent option is an errorless differential added reinforcement of other behaviors (errorless DRO) procedure, which then transitions to differential reinforcement of incompatible or alternative behaviors, once the initial disruptive emotional responding has been brought under control. This process is minimally invasive and achieves respondent counterconditioning as a byproduct, changing the emotional behaviors at the same time that operants are changed. This procedure is discussed in detail below (also see O'Heare, 2018a, 2018b).

Another option is Seligman's rehabilitation procedure, which is discussed in detail below.

Instate Training for Persistence/Industriousness, Creativity, and Resilience

Specific training exercises can be arranged to train specifically for persistence/industriousness, creativity, and/or emotional resilience. Each of these procedures is discussed in detail below. They may be instated broadly, or technologists may focus on particular ones, depending on what is needed for each case.

Changing Emotional Reactions to Aversive Stimulation

Emotional behaviors are respondent behaviors, and just as the intensity and likelihood of other conditioned respondents such as with salivating when a bell is rung, as in Pavlov's famous work, emotional reactions can be changed too.

Eliminating aversive emotional reactions generally means changing the emotional reaction—simply put, making the aversive stimulus no longer aversive. Emotional reactions to aversive stimuli, as respondents, can be changed via two different processes. The first is through the basic respondent conditioning pairing procedure, where an already established conditioned stimulus is involved as opposed to a neutral stimulus—a process called "respondent counterconditioning." The second is through respondent extinction, in which the conditioned stimulus is presented, but the unconditioned stimulus is not presented until the conditioned stimulus becomes neutral again. Respondent extinction, in its most common procedural form, is usually rather invasive and particularly problematic for individuals who already exhibit response depression and so this procedure is not elaborated nor generally recommended.

"Respondent counterconditioning" simply refers to respondent conditioning that counters or opposes previous conditioning—it causes a CS to elicit a CR that either cannot occur at the same time as the previously problematic CR that was displaced, or it simply opposes it, making the problem CR less intense. The procedure itself is a basic respondent conditioning procedure of pairing an NS with a US to increase the capacity of the NS (now a CS) to come to elicit the CR. It becomes *counter*conditioning when we take a CS that currently elicits aversive emotional arousal (inferred to occur based on signs of physiological stress and/or the occurrence of escape operants) and repeatedly pair it, not with the aversive US, but rather with an appetitive- or relaxation-eliciting stimulus instead. Gradually, the CS comes to elicit appetitive emotional arousal rather than aversive emotional arousal. Catania (2013, p. 436) put it this way: "Counterconditioning: in clinical applications, overcoming through new conditioning the effects of a CS that, by virtue of its relation to aversive US, has become aversive. Respondent contingencies involving a new CS are arranged so as to produce new CRs incompatible with those of the original conditioning."

It is not entirely clear to what extent respondent extinction is occurring during procedures commonly used to generate respondent counterconditioning but there certainly is more occurring than mere respondent extinction. When this procedure is taking place, the previously aversive unconditioned stimulus is not being presented and respondent extinction can be expected to take place as a result. However, the conditioned stimulus is also being paired with appetitive unconditioned stimuli and the result is not merely a reduction in aversive conditioned responding but an increase in appetitive emotional responding. Perhaps procedures used to generate respondent counterconditioning are complex arrangements involving respondent extinction and simultaneously the respondent conditioning of an appetitive emotional response. Alternatively, it may be the case that early in the process, extinction is occurring and as the procedure is repeated, new respondent conditioning takes over.

The respondent conditioning process described above is embodied in procedures called "systematic desensitization," sometimes simply referred to as "desensitization." These processes involve exposing the subject to stimuli in an incremental and graduated manner, such that the subject exhibits awareness-related behaviors with regard to the stimulus in question but does not, at this intensity, exhibit the aversive emotional reaction to the stimuli, and then pairing it with some appetitive rather than some unconditioned aversive stimulation, until the conditioned stimulus comes to elicit the appetitive rather than aversive emotional reaction. The broad and general term "desensitization" is often used to refer to this reduction in the aversive emotional reaction, largely because the term is purposely ambiguous with respect to exactly what is occurring in the conditioning process. Let's explore the topic in more depth, since it is at the heart of changing emotional behaviors

Respondent counterconditioning is achieved by presenting the aversive stimulus, followed by repeatedly presenting a stimulus that elicits a contrary emotional reaction, until the aversive stimulus ceases being aversive and the subject comes to react to it much as they would to the appetitive stimulus. The problem is that at full intensity, the subject sensitizes and counterconditioning becomes unlikely, and perhaps impossible (Mikulas, 1978). In order to achieve respondent counterconditioning, sensitization must be precluded. Therefore, *systematic desensitization* is composed of three steps:

- The subject is made to be relaxed, either actively in some way (mainly for humans) or by engaging in the procedure when the subject is already relaxed (mainly for non-humans).

- The aversive stimulus is broken down into a hierarchy of stimulus intensity along any of various dimensions ranked from least to most aversive.

- The subject is exposed, either via verbally guided imagination (*in vitro desensitization*—only for humans) or by actual contact with the aversive stimulus (*in vivo desensitization*—in the case of non-humans), to each successive stimulus intensity such that they do not sensitize, and once they are completely relaxed or experiencing appetitive emotional reactions at that level, the next level is instated and on until the subject can be exposed to the full intensity of the stimulus, with no indications of aversion emotional arousal being elicited.

Emotional reactions that might be tacted "anxiety" or "fear" are common kinds of aversive emotional arousal that are counterconditioned by either relaxation or appetitive emotional reactions (Mikulas, 1978). By working through the hierarchy of stimulus intensity, sensitization is prevented and the pairing procedure can take place. Remember, respondent extinction may also be occurring at least at first, but it is done without eliciting an aversive emotional reaction. The aversive stimulus is presented at such an intensity that it evokes attention and perhaps orientation, but not sensitization or any escape operants. Then, either the ongoing relaxation condition is paired with it or appetitive stimuli (e.g., treats, praise, toys, play, etc.) are paired with it and this is repeated until extinction and/or counterconditioning ("desensitization") occurs, and the subject comes to react to the problematic stimulus similarly to how they react to the stimuli that has been paired with it. This last change in behavior can only be explained by respondent counterconditioning, as opposed to respondent extinction.

In practice, it is rare that behaviorologists or technologists would refer to the procedure they utilize as "systematic desensitization," which is an old psychology term. Instead, the contingencies are externalized and the focus in placed on the operants. Behaviorologists and technologists might utilize an errorless DRO procedure to resolve escape behavior involving intense aversive stimulation. The errorless approach is used to ensure that the replacement behavior is likely to occur and the target behavior is not. The target behavior in such cases might be socially mediated escape (usually, aggressive behaviors) or direct escape (e.g., flight). In either case, the errorless approach allows the differential reinforcement procedure to occur without eliciting the problematic emotional behaviors or the target operant behaviors. The exposure to the aversive stimulus is broken down into a series of intensities such that the target behavior is not evoked and *any* behavior other than aggressive or flight behaviors are additively reinforced. Only once the subject reliably responds with desirable behaviors to the stimulus at the one level of intensity, is the level increased a small amount and further trials are carried out as in the previous level. In systematic desensitization, this exposure is referred to as a "hierarchy of stimulus intensity" and in an operant paradigm, it is simply an errorless approach to "fading in the evocative stimulus" and "differential reinforcement" of replacement behaviors. The result is the same. Whereas stimuli that elicit appetitive emotional responses are paired with the aversive stimulus under a respondent paradigm, in an operant paradigm, *other* operant behaviors are additively reinforced. The behavior can be anything other than the target behavior and since an errorless approach is used, the problematic behaviors will not occur. Since any operant at all is reinforced, this essentially means that the reinforcers will be presented at a high rate. Again, the appearance of the procedure and the behavioral result are the same under either paradigm. The difference is really only in the paradigm used to explain the conditioning processes occurring at the time—in other words, how we verbalize about the situation. Indeed, both kinds of conditioning are likely taking place. In the end, the "desensitization" occurs, no matter what explanation is exhibited. It is either conditioned directly or it occurs as a byproduct of the operant procedures. See the most current edition of my books *Aggressive Behavior in Dogs*, *Problem Animal Behavior*, or *Resolving Fears, Phobias, and Anxieties: An Errorless Differential Reinforcement Approach for Professionals* for elaboration of errorless DRO.

In summary, for cases involving aversive stimulation that cannot be simply forgone, the emotional reaction to the stimulus can be changed, thereby avoiding the side-effects common in exposure to this stimulation, including disempowerment, if the stimulus is not readily avoidable. A carefully arranged errorless DRO procedure can be used to change the emotional reaction as a byproduct of the operant conditioning processes. Changing the emotional reaction to aversive stimulation is an important means of eliminating aversive stimulation in cases where that stimulation cannot simply be prevented from occurring.

Rehabilitating Response Depression and Conditioned Helplessness in the Most Severe Cases

Seligman, Maier, and Geer (1968) posit that response depression, which they term "conditioned helplessness," is due to a conditioning history of response-consequence independence. The rehabilitation procedure that they devised involves establishing a conditioning history of response-consequence dependence—a high degree of contingency. In other words, if escape behaviors are currently not effective, there needs to be a history in which attempts to escape *are* successful. There is more than one way to apply this, but I start with the approach Seligman and colleagues described.

Seligman and colleagues (1968) demonstrated that the following intervention successfully rehabilitated dogs exhibiting conditioned helplessness.

First, they exposed the dogs to inescapable shocks to produce conditioned helplessness and confirmed a persistent response depression. Next, they instated a two-phase intervention. Phase 1 involved putting the dogs back into their shuttle box, but this time lowering the barricade to be jumped in order to escape the shocks to a mere 12.7 cm (5 inches). When the trials began, the door was opened and the experimenter verbally prompted the dogs to the other side. One of the four dogs responded to the prompt and successfully escaped, avoiding the shocks. The remaining dogs went on to phase 2, in which leashes were attached to the dogs' necks and they were literally dragged to the other side of the barricade and to safety. In some cases, it took many trials before the dogs began exhibiting the escape behaviors themselves. Following phase 2, each dog was exposed to a "recovery" phase of further escape/avoidance training. The interventions were very successful in getting the dogs behaving again and, specifically, behaving in order to escape the aversive stimulation.

Inoculation Against Conditioned Helplessness and Response Depression

Seligman followed up his research on conditioned helplessness with work on alleviating it once it is established. Later, he discussed the idea of "conditioned optimism" and inoculation against conditioned helplessness effects. The strategies that Seligman developed for inoculation against conditioned helplessness can involve forcing contact with aversive stimuli. Seligman and Maier (1967) found that prior exposure to escapable aversive stimulation reduces future response depression in inescapable aversive situations. Therefore, effective escape conditioning can inoculate animals against passivity effects in the face of aversive stimulation.

Although safety stimulation procedures are described, their usefulness is limited to instances in which aversive stimulation cannot be forgone or where errorless DRO procedures can be used to change the emotional reaction, as opposed to just warning that the aversive is not coming. I have yet to see a case for which an errorless shaping or DRO procedure that emphasizes contingency and empowerment-related behaviors of behavior (e.g., persistence/industriousness, creativity, resilience) was impossible or inadequate. But, for the sake of completeness and because it might indeed prove necessary in rare instances, I discuss it here. Regardless, the focus of most rehabilitation programs should be placed on forgoing aversive stimulation or changing the emotional reactions to aversive stimulation.

Safety Stimulation and its Influence on Empowerment

As we have seen, controllability plays an extremely important role in response depression versus empowerment. Predictability is also important. Being able to predict aversive stimulation can attenuate detrimental response depression effects, likely by attenuating fear, although there are other hypotheses for the mechanisms involved (Maier & Warren, 1988). By attenuating fear, technologists increase the likelihood of escape responding—which is both subtractively reinforced (Brennan, Beck & Servatius 2003) and additively reinforced (Dinsmoor, 2001)—and thereby avoid many of the behavioral deficits associated with response depression.

Predictability can be generated with a “safety” stimulus.[11] A safety stimulus is a stimulus that is presented when a period of time is about to start in which *no* aversive stimulus will be delivered. It is used in circumstances in which the subject will occasionally be exposed to aversers—in others words, where aversers will sometimes be present and sometimes not. The stimulus allows the subject to predict the non-aversive occasions. By predicting safety from aversive stimulation, the safety stimulus allows for relief and minimizes emotional arousal, which, in turn, sets the occasion for quick and effective escape behavior rather than response depression at times when the averser is present. “Just as stimuli directly or positively correlated with the delivery of shock become aversive to the [subject], so stimuli inversely or negatively correlated with the shock (safety signals) become positive reinforcers” (Dinsmoor, 2001).

Maier and Warren (1988) demonstrated that safety stimulation effectively reduces the impact of aversers delivered in the same session, but not with aversers delivered in subsequent sessions. The safety stimulus can be useful for minimizing emotional arousal during sessions in which it is used, but may

[11] The original term is “safety signal,” but the use of the word signal is problematic as it implies communication theory common within psychology which is eschewed by behaviorologists. I will use the term “safety stimulus” as it is accurate without the agential “baggage.”

not be useful as an immunization against subsequent aversive occasions. Longer safety stimulation duration intervals are associated with less anxiety than shorter durations (Brennan, Beck & Servatius 2003). See Dinsmoor (2001) for a discussion of competing hypotheses regarding safety stimulation and aversive conditioning more generally.

The safety stimulus can be useful when aversive events are unavoidable, and the goal is to minimize the intensity of their impact and prevent a high degree of aversive arousal. In these situations, the goal is to reduce stress and emotional arousal and to promote quick and effective escape responding, which then reduces the aversiveness of the training situation.

For those of us dedicated to non-aversive methods, it might be difficult to recall an example of wanting to protect our training from aversers in this way. One example is the use of a safety stimulus in cases when the subject becomes anxious and panics in response to diminished social contact (i.e., "separation anxiety"). It is not always possible to remain with the subject at all times throughout the behavior change project. A safety stimulus is used during trials when the subject will *not* be exposed to diminished social contact. This allows the subject to be calmer when there will be no diminished social contact, reducing the general emotionality and the sensitization effect and it functions to protect, to some degree, the conditioning carried out at that time. Another situation in which it might be used is during protracted periods of repeated aversive medical interventions. In all cases, the safety stimulus can be faded later.

Specific Empowerment Rehabilitation Tactics

Persistence Training to Inoculate Against and Rehabilitate Depressed Responding

Persistence training seeks to improve the persistence of adaptive behaviors within the context of a general behavior change project. It is specifically intended to help address situations in which the subject's repertoire is narrowed or where adaptive behaviors are depressed due to a history of noncontingent response-consequence conditioning, including inescapable aversive stimulation.

Much behaviorally-oriented training to rehabilitate helpless or response-depressed individuals has emphasized "success training" (Nation & Massad, 1978), which seems putatively useful. This has focused on continuous response-contingent reinforcement paradigms. Unfortunately, although rapid success can be achieved, this approach poses a significant risk of post-intervention relapse (Nation & Woods, 1980).

It is not enough to improve behavioral well-being by simply increasing the volume of response-contingent added reinforcement the subject contacts, setting them up for repeated and continuous success. What happens outside of the training setting when that individual fails to achieve instant gratification? That is, what happens when not everything "goes their way" after this 100% success training? Inevitable extinction trials (i.e., failures) usually result in a relapse, resilience deteriorates, and frustration increases. The individual was not prepared for failure. In fact, the subject was set up the worst kind of failure, which causes a problem worse than the one present before the procedure. Individuals must be prepared to manage challenges with persistence and resilience. To achieve long-term behavioral well-being, the subject must be conditioned to exhibit effective strategies for meeting challenges and overcoming frustrations. Creativity, persistence, and resilience are of paramount importance in this regard. A well-established body of work is available for promoting such long-term objectives.

Tolerance of frustrating outcomes is a key feature of empowerment. Nation and Woods (1980) point to research indicating that "failure manipulation judiciously arranged," so-called failure training ("failure applied contingently along with success"), can promote persistence, whereas behaviors trained solely in an errorless system may be less resistant to extinction. In this training, criterion behaviors (i.e., behaviors that would otherwise meet the criteria for delivery of the reinforcer) intermittently result in non-reinforcement. The training is carried out in an incremental, graded manner after a solid foundation of response-contingent added reinforcement-based success training (Nation & Woods, 1980). This process is familiar to animal trainers as "thinning the schedule of reinforcement."

In the early stages, subjects are set up for success, and in the later stages, they are gradually set up for minor failures, or "disappointment," at a level that allows them to "expect" occasional non-reinforcement and to overcome it. This then sets them up for a more adaptive, longer-term, kind of success. Persistence, or behaviors associated with keeping at a task, can be reinforced. Again, this requires careful attention to ensuring that the subject keeps working and does not become discouraged and give up. The failures need to be used in such a way that they increase continued working to contact the reinforcer, but not in a way that will damage confidence. This requires effective training judgment. Solving complex training problems can be extremely empowering and overcoming challenges and failures can be a big part of why this works so well. However, managed poorly, it can have the opposite effect and reduce empowerment!

The emphasis is on framing the behavior change project in such a way that the adaptive behavior persists, post-intervention, in the "real world" where failure and extinction can be expected to occur. This training tactic might simply be thought of as a behavior change program with more effective maintenance tactics. Nation, Cooney, and Cartrell (1979) studied the durability and generalizability of persistence in their persistence-training model. They define durability, as it relates to the partial reinforcement extinction effect (PREE), as "the capacity of acquired behaviors to endure successive episodes of extinction and reacquisition." They define generalizability as "a transfer of learning phenomenon that is defined relative to the probability that learned events will appear as topographically different behaviors across a broad range of situations." These authors found that durability and generalizability were stronger when intermittent reinforcement was used during persistence training than when continuous reinforcement was used. Nation and Massad (1978) and Nation and Woods (1980) proposed the following four steps in persistence training:

- identification of coping behaviors;
- acquisition training with continuous reinforcement;
- training with intermittent reinforcement; and
- periodic adjustment.

Each point is elaborated upon below.

Identification of Coping Behaviors

The first step is to select behaviors. In some cases, these may merely be "tricks" or other fun behaviors that are trained to provide the opportunity to instate a highly contingent response-consequence relationship and rehabilitate depressed responding. The immunizing effects against further conditioned helplessness is expected to generalize, as is effort and creativity conditioning.

In other cases, where specific behaviors are required, as in replacing problem behaviors, select behaviors that will be topographically similar to what will be required later, outside of the formal training environment (Nation & Massad, 1978).

Acquisition Training with Continuous Reinforcement

The next step involves training the specified behaviors through the initial acquisition phase. Start with continuous reinforcement for this step to ensure a high degree of contingency. The goal at this stage is to arrange the environment to allow for success on each trial in an errorless manner. A high density of reinforcement is desirable here. Continuous reinforcement—a high density of reinforcement and a high degree of contingency—is well suited, not only to the initial acquisition phase, but also to rehabilitate conditioned helplessness by establishing a strong causal relationship between behavior and consequences; this relationship is absent in conditioned helplessness or depressed responding (Nation & Massad, 1978).

Where problematic emotional arousal involved, such as in those cases labeled with "fear" or "anxiety," is disruptive to training, an errorless approach is vital. In this approach, you arrange the environment to prevent elicitation of the problematic emotional behaviors or evocation of problematic/non-criterion behaviors, and gradually expose the subject to the added reinforcement contingencies in question. You ensure that the behavior of concern is highly likely and any problematic behaviors (usually escape related) are highly unlikely. The key feature of this step is ensuring that the subject is successful in developing new adaptive behaviors to replace maladaptive behaviors (Nation & Massad, 1978).

Training with Intermittent Reinforcement

The progressive intermittent reinforcement step is specifically designed to promote durable and generalizable persistence—to take a strongly conditioned behavior and immunize it against relapse/deterioration after training during everyday extinction trials. In the "real world" (i.e., environments that are not pre-planned and highly controlled), not all occurrences of behavior will be reinforced. This can be particularly problematic for animals who have experienced some level of depressed responding (and indeed for those who have had nothing but 100% success thus far, something you might recognize from the "spoiled child" effect).

They will readily become frustrated, and their responding will be depressed again, unless persistence is conditioned.

In this step, progressively stretched intermittent schedules of added reinforcement are put in place for the training. As Nation and Massad (1978) point out, it is not failure per se, that we promote. We do not set the subject up for non-criterion behaviors (i.e., behaviors that do not satisfy the established criteria for reinforcement delivery). Instead, we continue to set the subject up for success and put the criterion behavior on an intermittent schedule, taking advantage of the partial reinforcement effect. Lattal, Reilly, and Kohn (1998) showed that behaviors maintained on interval schedules of added reinforcement may persist longer than behaviors maintained on ratio schedules of added reinforcement. Where feasible, consider using interval schedules in some training. The schedule should be thinned gradually and progressively, ideally in a variable, rather than fixed fashion. This will mean that some correct behaviors will fail to generate the expected reinforcement. These failures come to elicit minimal aversion because of the otherwise rich schedule of added reinforcement.

Some animal trainers have argued for using a continuous reinforcement schedule rather than an intermittent schedule in later stages of training and even maintenance. Indeed, if one were training the behavior in question for a controlled and specific task such as performance of an unusual behavior in a TV commercial, continuous reinforcement would be a quick and easy way to establish the behavior. In this case, one is not concerned about maintenance of the behavior in the long term in dynamic environments where extinction trials will be necessary and unavoidable. In the "real world," one needs the persistence and durability effects that intermittent schedules provide.

Do not rush this step. Nation and Massad (1978) demonstrated that extended work at this stage of the program promotes greater durability and generalizability of the persistence effects. The most extensive work should be put into behaviors that are expected to contact greater extinction contingencies later. Furthermore, on top of Nation and Massad's plan, work in training specifically for greater effort and use training methods such as shaping to promote creativity. This is discussed further below.

Periodic Adjustment

Adaptive behaviors that are conditioned in persistence training may not necessarily access intrinsic reinforcers as readily as problem behaviors have in the animal's past experience. It is important, after the intervention stage of training, to periodically refresh the conditioning and make any necessary adjustments to take into account any new contexts that might be in place.

Industriousness Training

Industriousness relates to effort (i.e., energy expenditure) and can be promoted by establishing effort as part of the reinforcement criteria. Furthermore, research shows that effort can generalize. Reinforcing effort in some training tasks can promote increased effort in other behaviors. Eisenberger and colleagues (1982) and Eisenberger (1992) coined the term "learned industriousness" to refer to conditioning that promotes persistence and increased effort. They found that reinforcing increased effort generalizes and that you can train a "try strategy," as they called it (Eisenberger & Leonard, 1980; Eisenberger et al., 1982; Eisenberger et al., 1983).

The first and most obvious procedure for increasing industriousness is simply to reinforce it. This means working toward criteria for reinforcement that involve effort. One can shape more industrious behaving by incrementally requiring greater response effort in specific training tasks.

Other measures found to increase industriousness include increasing the variety of training tasks and the response effort required to exhibit these varied tasks. This should generalize to other contingencies and promote the "try strategy," generally a good strategy for contacting reinforcers (Eisenberger, 1980, 1982, 1983). Train behaviors that are challenging but manageable (Eisenberger, 1982; Nation & Woods, 1980). This means finding the "sweet spot" between boring and frustrating. This takes a bit of experience, careful observation, and some good judgment (i.e., discrimination training), but you can expand your repertoire of effective training behaviors by observing carefully for feedback (i.e., consequences) on your training behaviors by quantifying the changes.

Another tactic for increasing industriousness is to ensure occasional failures that the subject then overcomes. "Initial failure on assigned tasks serves as a cue to work harder" (Eisenberger, 1982). Notice that this is about *trying harder* rather than *keeping trying*, which differentiates industriousness from persistence.

Creativity Training: Shaping Creativity, Persistence and Resilience

"Creativity" as a general behavioral tendency can also be conditioned. Shaping is an excellent training procedure for promoting empowerment, not only because it allows one to train complex behaviors that could not otherwise be trained and because it can be done in a non-coercive manner, but also because it promotes the general behavioral tactics that make up empowerment: creativity; industriousness/persistence; and resilience. When implemented well, it provides the subject with seeming "power and control." Achieving all of these effects in one training procedure makes shaping the most powerful tool available for promoting empowerment and behavioral well-being in general. As Fraley (2008) puts it: "Because *creativity* is defined as the production of novel yet worthwhile products, the differential reinforcement procedure [in this case, shaping] is an important aspect of the behavioral technology for training people [and members of other species] to be more creative."

Shaping is not a panacea; it will not solve all instances of response depression on its own. One cannot ignore the promotion of empowerment in other parts of the subject's life and believe that shaping will "cure" disempowerment. However, shaping has greater beneficial effects on empowerment than any other single procedure of which I am aware.

Shaping is a procedure that involves the differential reinforcement of *successive approximations* of a target behavior. Shaping is a special type of differential reinforcement. All differential reinforcement procedures change the *rate* of a target behavior. Shaping changes the *form* of a terminal behavior, making it a unique type of differential reinforcement. Shaping involves a series of standard (i.e., rate-changing) differential reinforcement procedures carried out in succession. One increases the rate of an approximation of the terminal behavior through differential reinforcement, and then uses the same process with another, closer, approximation to the terminal behavior. This process is repeated until the subject exhibits the terminal behavior. The *rate* of each approximation is increased one at a time, allowing for training the next approximation until the terminal behavior *form* is achieved.

Where the target behavior occurs frequently enough or can readily be prompted in its final form, standard differential reinforcement is used. If the target behavior does not occur in its final form frequently enough or cannot be readily prompted in its final form, shaping is used.

Not every response is precisely the same. This variability in the different properties of a response class from one occurrence to another facilitates selection and reinforcement of some variations over others. The initial approximation is set such that it will occur frequently enough for the trainer to reinforce it. The uncontrived environment may evoke the approximation, or the trainer may prompt it. Once that response class form has a history of reinforcement, it will occur more frequently. Then, that response class form is put on extinction in favor of the next approximation. A common byproduct of extinction is increased behavioral variability. Ensure that the second approximation is set such that it will fall within the range of variant response class forms resulting from the extinction process. In other words, the next approximation cannot be too different from the one that was just established. This new approximation is then targeted for reinforcement and its rate is increased. The shaping process continues until the subject exhibits the terminal behavior fluently. We refer to this reiteration through cycles of differentially reinforcing approximations toward a terminal behavior form as "shaping."

Shaping is a postcedent procedure because it manipulates what comes *after* the behavior. That is, shaping involves manipulating consequences in order to change the likelihood of the behavior on subsequent occasions. Shaping, itself, does not specify any antecedent conditions; it does not specify whether a trainer-mediated stimulus evokes the behavior or not. The somewhat colloquial term "free-shaping" indicates a shaping program in which prompting is avoided.

There is value in avoiding prompts in some shaping projects, particularly when the trainer is attempting to reinforce creativity and persistence in general, as well as the specific behavior in question. One benefit of promptless shaping is that no prompt needs to be faded. Another benefit, expressed somewhat agentially, is that it provides the subject with greater behavioral "freedom" and a wider range of options. In other words, creativity and persistence are reinforced, along with the specific behavior of concern. With increased creativity and persistence, individuals exhibit behavioral tendencies and strategies that allow them to contact an increased number of reinforcers and their general behavioral well-being is improved. These effects or byproducts are what some trainers are referring to when they colloquially say that animals that are free-shaped are "smarter" for it. The subject is conditioned to approach problems (e.g., obstructed access to reinforcers—that is, frustrating circumstances), by behaving experimentally with productive novel behaviors rather than behaving rigidly and then becoming emotionally "unglued" or depressed when their behaviors fail to generate reinforcement. When their contact with reinforcers is obstructed, they persist, rather than giving up easily and respond with less emotionality, which commonly generates behaviors that interfere with training.

There are some limitations to shaping of which trainers should be aware. Cooper and colleagues (2007, p. 425) point out that shaping can be time consuming, that progress through approximations is often erratic rather than linear and smooth, that the trainer must be extremely attentive for indications of a need to change criteria, and that shaping can be misapplied and promote problem behaviors.

Shaping requires excellent timing, and so a conditioned added reinforcer is used. Various products can be used as conditioned added reinforcers; a clicker is very useful for this purpose. Here are a few tips for using the clicker:

- Always follow the click with an unconditioned reinforcer.

- Do not use the clicker for any purpose other than as a conditioned added reinforcer. Do not, for instance, use the same click stimulus for a conditioned added reinforcer and for a conditioned subtracted reinforcer, a conditioned subtracted punisher, a safety stimulus or a so-called "keep-going" stimulus. If you wish to use a keep-going stimulus, use a completely different conditioned stimulus for that purpose.

- When you put the reinforcement on an intermittent schedule, put the click and the unconditioned reinforcer on the same schedule—every time you click, provide the "treat." Avoid clicking and failing to deliver the "treat." Adhering to this rule will allow you to maintain the highest degree of contingency and the greatest strength of reinforcement.

- Start with a single kind of unconditioned reinforcer but then begin using multiple different unconditioned reinforcers, so that the clicker will act as a generalized conditioned reinforcer. This will allow you a bit more flexibility in using the clicker because you will not have to worry as much about satiation with the unconditioned reinforcer.

Shaping Procedure

The procedure outlined below is a guide to conducting a shaping program from beginning to end:

- Determine the terminal response class form.

- Determine the conditioned and unconditioned reinforcers.

- Determine approximations.
- Implement the shaping program.
- When the target behavior is achieved, establish a cue.
- Program for maintenance.

Determine Terminal Response Class Form

The first step in a shaping program is to select the terminal response class form. In problem behavior cases, this will usually be a replacement behavior. Define the terminal response class form with specificity, this is not the time to be vague. Remember that response class forms not only identify the function of the behavior, but also specify the specific structural or form criteria that must be met. You also need to identify the measurement criterion for occurrence of the behavior. It might be a specific rate or relative frequency, and it might require a specific magnitude or duration as well. This is your behavior objective.

Determine Conditioned and Unconditioned Reinforcers

Once you have identified your behavior objective, you should identify the conditioned and unconditioned reinforcers you will use. For conditioned reinforcers, clickers are readily available and work well. If you prefer a spoken word instead of a clicker, the conditioning may not be as precise as if you used a crisp and unique sound that is used only for training purposes and that can be activated very rapidly. On the other hand, using a word is more intuitive and can be more easily managed by some trainers while leashes and treats are also being manipulated.

For an unconditioned reinforcer, there are sophisticated ways of deciding which to use. Generally, most guardians will be able to inform you quite readily on the subject's few most effective reinforcers under most conditions. It might be treats, which are ideal because they are quick and easy to deliver without disrupting momentum, or it might be praise and touch for some subjects (and definitely not for some others), or it might be playing (a quick toss of a toy or game of tug).

Once training is well under way, vary the unconditioned reinforcers to promote a generalized reinforcement.

If you restrict access to the unconditioned reinforcer to establish greater effectiveness, do not deprive the subject too heavily as this can have a detrimental effect.

Determine Approximations

Determining the approximations to the terminal response class form requires careful judgment and flexibility in implementing the training steps. Find a subject of the same species (and similar breed perhaps) who already exhibits the behavior. Either observe them exhibit the behavior or, better yet, video-record it and watch it repeatedly, perhaps in slow motion. This will allow you to prepare a list of approximations. If this is not possible, visualize the behavior occurring and prepare your list based on this. With experience, you will become very familiar with the approximations to use for common terminal response class forms. The first approximation must occur frequently enough to provide adequate opportunity to reinforce the behavior, and each approximation needs to make the next approximation likely to occur frequently enough to build on also. If you have to wait too long for the behavior to occur, conditioning will be extremely slow, if it occurs at all, and will likely be frustrating for both the trainer and the subject. In a relatively brief first session, you will want the behavior to occur several times. Prompt where necessary but avoid prompting where possible.

It is very important that the approximations are not too small or too large. Ensure that the approximations are small enough to avoid quick satiation and maintain a smooth pace, without leading to significant frustration. If the approximation is too large, the subject will become frustrated (involving aversive emotional arousal) or bored and distracted (i.e., too sparse a schedule of added reinforcement leads to other contingencies exerting power over the subject's behavior). If the approximations are too small, not much creativity will be required, and you will find that the subject will frequently jump through several approximations; this can present a challenge to the trainer. Err on the side of smaller approximations, because frustration is more disruptive to training than the alternative. The approximations should be as gradual as possible, so that training moves smoothly from approximation to approximation.

The approximations, including the terminal response class form, should be written down in a clear list. This list will be your guide to training but remain flexible. It is important to have a prepared plan for shaping programs to ensure that you are prepared for each approximation when it occurs.

Implement Shaping Program

Once you have prepared your shaping program, it is time to implement it. Implementing a shaping program involves a complex repertoire of skills, requiring quick and effective judgment, usually based on significant experience. It is definitely an advanced training procedure to carry out effectively and efficiently. Remember, a poorly executed shaping program can be frustrating for the subject (as well as the trainer).

If the training is going smoothly and you are on track, you will experience very few extinction trials or long periods of time in which there are no responses or the subject is attending elsewhere. If, on the other hand, the subject is losing interest, exhibiting very few behaviors or exhibiting non-criterion behaviors, then you are likely not moving at an appropriate pace. If you move too slowly, you risk the subject "losing interest" (i.e., the contingencies do not generate adequate added reinforcers to maintain the subject's participation and they are likely to attend to competing contingencies in the environment). If you move too quickly, you may begin to get a greater number of extinction trials and higher levels of frustration. When beginning an approximation, there will be extinction trials necessarily, but if you set the approximations appropriately there should be very few. You should quickly progress to 100% reinforcement trials.

If you reach a challenging part and the subject becomes frustrated, it can be useful to take a break. Toss a treat to change the focus temporarily away from the contingency at hand. Take the time to identify the variables that are causing the problem, so that you can fix them. Perhaps call the subject to you, request a simple previously well-conditioned behavior, and provide an enthusiastic reinforcement package (treats, praise, and energy). If need be, take a small break to do something different, be it fun or relaxing before proceeding again.[12] Occasionally, it seems as though a "frustration loop" develops and has the potential to deteriorate the training. Taking a very brief break can be immensely helpful in this respect. If a subject responds to training with escape behavior, this bodes very poorly for effective training. If that occurs, you will need to take it very slowly, ensure success at first and ensure it is fun.

It is important to remain at any particular approximation long enough to establish fluency but not longer. Mastery and maintenance are reserved for the terminal behavior. Moving to the next approximation before fluency is achieved will result in a greater number of extinction trials in following approximations, and frustration will result. Remaining at an approximation too long will result in too strong conditioning at that approximation, which will require more extinction of that behavior at the next approximation. A good rule of thumb is that the training in any given approximation should be progressing smoothly. Where it is not, adjustments need to be made.

When you move to the next approximation, if that behavior is not exhibited quickly, you need to be flexible. There is something to be said for allowing the subject to "figure it out" on their own; that is how they become conditioned to exhibit persistence and creativity. However, if it goes on for too long, the subject can become frustrated and then eventually response-depressed instead, which is particularly important when dealing with disempowered or response depressed subjects. If the subject does not exhibit

[12] Always be on the lookout for subtractively reinforced behaviors that will be disruptive to training. If a non-criterion behavior results in an end to a session that is aversive, you can expect that behavior to increase, which will be a behavior that is disruptive to training. The goal is for training to be reinforcing. If it is not, your area of focus should be solving this problem. Also, keep training fun, so that escape behaviors are irrelevant!

the behavior quickly, you can go back to the previous approximation, carry out several trials of it and then insert an intermediate approximation (a sub-step, so to speak). This will allow you to continue progressing. Having a plan will make it easier for you to quickly come up with intermediate approximations when needed.

When Target Behavior is Achieved, Establish a Cue

Once the terminal response class form has been achieved and is stable, it is time to transfer stimulus control to a specific cue. In order to establish a cue for this new behavior, discrimination training is carried out. Initially, deliver the cue immediately before the behavior is exhibited. Repeat this sequence through several trials. Continue, at this early stage, to reinforce the behavior even when it is not cued, but once it becomes smooth and reliable begin reinforcing only when the cue is delivered and not otherwise. Soon the new cue will take on stimulus control over the behavior.

The cue does not always have to be a vocal cue. You could make some specific situation cue the behavior. In many behavior change projects, we transfer stimulus control to the stimulus that previously evoked the problem behavior (hence the term "replacement behavior"). If this is done, an errorless approach should be implemented, such that the stimulus is presented at incrementally more salient exposure intensities without the subject exhibiting the problem behavior.

Program for Maintenance

Once the terminal response class form is on a progressively thinning intermittent schedule of added reinforcement and it is being exhibited on cue—rather than any time you pick up your clicker for example—you can begin conducting trials in different environments, including increasingly distracting ones with competing contingencies, in order to promote setting generalization and effective discrimination. If it has not already been done, begin using various unconditioned reinforcers. In particular, use activities (e.g,, Premack) reinforcers in the environment and praise so that the behavior is sustainable in the long run.

These final two steps are not always necessary, particularly when you are shaping simply for the creativity and persistence benefits and it is the process, rather than the product, that is fundamentally important.

Troubleshooting with Shaping

It is difficult to provide guidelines for good trainer judgment because there are so many important variables at play, but remember that shaping is really all about discrimination and generalization. Shaping is a fast-paced balancing act, in which the trainer manages frustration and success, making quick adjustments to the schedules of reinforcement and the success criteria on a moment-by-moment basis.

Furthermore, every subject is different. Some subjects behave rigidly and become frustrated after even 3 seconds of no reinforcement. Others "enthusiastically" exhibit a long string of behaviors that have had histories of added reinforcement.

These are challenging obstacles to overcome. Effective judgment and technique-implementation in working through these challenges are important for success in training, and in particular, shaping for empowerment. Avoid working on shaping programs with subjects who are disempowered or easily frustrated until you have worked with subjects of the same species who are only mildly disempowered, so that you are well prepared. Below are a few pieces of advice to help work through some common problems that arise in shaping programs.

Approximation Steps Too Large

One of the most common errors in shaping programs is requiring too large a step between approximations. If the step is too large, meaning that the topographic difference between the previous criterion and the new criterion is too high, the subject will be less likely to exhibit that next criterion frequently enough to build on without periods of extinction and frustration or boredom/distraction. Extinction generates topographic behavioral variability, and it is from these variable response class forms the next approximation is selected. If your next approximation is not a likely variation, you will not achieve reinforceable responses. It is vital, especially in the context of promoting empowerment, that the steps are large enough that there is actually something to "figure out" (so to speak) but small enough to prevent excessive frustration or boredom/distraction (i.e., intrusive competing contingencies).

The difference between frustration and boredom is related to the relative effectiveness of the reinforcers used in a particular contingency. If the reinforcers are highly effective, extinction will be frustrating, whereas if the reinforcers are less effective, extinction will produce boredom. Competing contingencies that make available more highly effective reinforcers produce distraction. Manage distraction and observe the subject carefully for indications of frustration. The subject may vocalize, begin to "give up," "shut down," or exhibit seemingly out-of-context behaviors. At the very first indications of stress, frustration, or boredom, make adjustments to resolve the problem quickly. Keep the subject in the game, trying, and having fun. This is usually managed with the size of the approximation, the effectiveness of the reinforcers, and the pace and social enthusiasm the trainer applies.

If the subject is engaging in behaviors involving outside contingencies, take control of these extraneous reinforcers and also increase the effectiveness of the reinforcers you are utilizing in your training. This might involve increasing your enthusiasm and quickening the pace a little. If competing contingencies are interfering with training, change the environment in a way that will get things back on track.

If the subject becomes frustrated, usually the best solution is to go back to the previous approximation, achieve a series of successful trials and insert a sub-step between that approximation and the next one. In other words, find a smaller approximation, which will set both of you up for success.

Smaller steps, a higher degree of contingency, better timing, and more enthusiasm are often called for to prevent frustration, but it all depends on the individual subject. Be receptive, observant, flexible, and responsive.

Not Reinforcing Frequently Enough or Too Many Extinction Trials

If you find that you are administering too many extinction trials, either because a non-criterion behavior is exhibited or the subject exhibits no specific behaviors for an extended period of time, you have a problem. The pace should move as smoothly as possible and excessive frustration should be prevented. Make quick adjustments on the fly to improve the rate of reinforcement. This might mean inserting a prompt to generate a reinforceable behavior or relaxing the criteria and building the behavior back up. In some cases, it can mean *mild* deprivation to establish the effectiveness of the reinforcer or breaking for another activity and coming back to the training later.

Remember that shaping is a balancing act; it should be challenging enough to set the occasion for creativity and persistence, but not so challenging that minor frustration that turns to frustration and response depression. *Always* err on the side of preventing frustration. A brief, well-placed prompt can be helpful. Often, throwing a treat to a location can prompt the subject. Sometimes even just looking at or gesturing to a location can help. Sometimes a few words of encouragement will get the job done. Avoid physical prompts, as they are often disruptive to training. Sometimes, all you need is to become a bit more animated and enthusiastic in order to generate greater arousal and hence a greater number of behaviors from which to select.

Shaping Tips

Here are some tips that will help you improve your shaping skills:

- Define your terminal response class form clearly and operationally, including a specific measure for it. Don't settle for vague characterizations or unverifiable mental states.

- Prepare a shaping plan ahead of time, identifying each approximation, as a guide, but remain flexible. Be prepared to break an approximation down into more steps if the subject "jumps" steps.

Also, be prepared to end a session early after a series of successful trials, so that the process remains a pleasant experience.

- Identify highly effective reinforcers and, where necessary, use *mild* appropriate deprivation to increase their effectiveness. Use a clicker or other precise, clear, and unique stimulus as your conditioned reinforcer. Maintain the best timing and contiguity possible.

- Set approximations large enough that the conditioning is not likely to jump more than a couple of steps at a time, but small enough to prevent frustration or boredom/distraction. Monitor throughout for necessary adjustments.

- Shape one clear dimension of the behavior at a time as your approximation criterion (e.g., duration, frequency, or latency). When shaping another dimension, initially relax the other dimensions.

- ***Always have fun, and make sure the subject does too***! Maintain enthusiasm, and a demeanor and pace appropriate for the subject. Avoid interruptions and distractions. Pay close attention to the subject, and do not become distracted yourself. You do have an ultimate goal but remain in the moment, to ensure that the process is fun at every stage.

- If the rate or frequency of the behavior deteriorates or fails to progress adequately, review previous approximations, and consider pace and enthusiasm or even a different behavior or training method.

- End training sessions after a series of successfully reinforced trials rather than after extinction trials (i.e., end on a good note). Be very observant for any initial indications of frustration or boredom and try to end before these occur in subsequent sessions. If necessary, provide reinforcers for a few trials at a previous approximation before ending.

- When beginning a new session, review at the previous approximation and work past where you ended your last session, rather than picking up where you left off before.

- Maintain consistency in as many areas of the training environment as possible, except the approximation levels, until it is time to work toward maintenance. This includes using the same trainer and training in the same location with the same reinforcers. Generalization and discrimination training can be achieved later, once the terminal response class form is achieved.

Free-shaping Games

Below are some suggested shaping games. These games will help you hone your shaping skills.

Shaping a Friend

You will need a clicker and at least two people for the exercise (although it is more fun with three or more), as well as reinforcers (e.g., quarters or some other physical object that can be given to the subject in order to simulate treat delivery). You will also need a piece of paper and writing instrument for the planning stage.

This exercise is an excellent way to practice shaping without subjecting a companion animal to the frustration and confusion often associated with novice trainers carrying out an advanced training procedure. It is largely based on an excellent game (the Training Game) described in *Don't Shoot the Dog* by Karen Pryor, with the addition of a concerted shaping plan before the game.

There are two projects in this exercise, one in which you are the trainer and the other in which you are the subject. In the first project, your friend is the subject and you are the trainer. The subject leaves the room for the planning stage. Identify an operationalized behavior to train the subject to exhibit.

Write down your target behavior and prepare a plan of approximations just as you would if you were planning a training project.

Once you have a plan, have the subject come back into the room and you begin the training. No speaking or contrived prompting, including subtle head nods and noises or other facial expressions are allowed. You can justify occasional prompts in this exercise in order to work through a particularly frustrating series of trials but try not to use them unless you absolutely need to in order to be successful. Rather, focus on preventing the need for them—working through these challenges with adjustments to approximation size and pace.

Note that it is often necessary to get your friend to a specific place for the behavior to occur. Take note that this is really a separate behavior and hence there is also forward chaining taking place as well. With humans, it is usually quite clear that getting to a specific spot comes before the behavior that being in that spot requires. Under these circumstances, it is usually appropriate to shape the movement behavior and then shape the terminal response class form once at the appropriate spot because this is such a simple sequence of discrete behaviors.

Click for successive approximations of the terminal response class form in accordance with your training plan but be prepared to adjust your tactics, where appropriate. Maintain a high rate of reinforcement to ensure smooth training and minimal frustration or confusion for the subject. In place of the unconditioned reinforcer, give the subject quarters or some other physical reinforcer for this exercise to simulate treat delivery. When the subject finally exhibits the terminal behavior, the game is over.

Remember to click frequently and set the approximations small enough that the subject does not become frustrated, but large enough that they maintain momentum and do not get bored. By far, the most common cause of problems in this game is using too sparse a schedule of reinforcement. In other words, the trainer sets too large of approximations and this results in trainee frustration. You should be reinforcing at least every few seconds.

Dealing with treat delivery will usually take up more time than waiting for approximations.

Take turns being the trainer, the subject and even a non-participating observer. This kind of game can generate a great deal of trainer skill conditioning. Attend carefully to indications of frustration and boredom and to superstitious and adjunctive behaviors for conditioning experiences.

When you have finished, contemplate what has been conditioned in your repertoire of training skills and ask the subject about their experience with the training. Did the subject become frustrated or bored? How could you have prevented that? Usually, you can prevent frustration with smaller approximations and more frequent reinforcement. Did the subject seemingly exhibit and repeat superstitious behaviors? How could you work through this kind of behavior? Usually, the best way is to go back a couple of approximations and start again, this time being sure to reinforce instances of the correct approximation but without the superstitious behavior. Avoid reinforcing superstitious behavior. Sometimes, you will need to use a brief prompt to get past a problem and prevent frustration. Often, intruding superstitious behaviors indicate too sparse a reinforcement schedule. In these cases, the subject is left to guess at what behavior to exhibit rather than simply exhibiting what has been reinforced.

Identify at least three things you could improve and how you will improve them.

Free-shaping with a Box

This game is based, with some minor adjustments, on Karen Pryor's game called "101 Things To Do With a Box" (Pryor, 2009).

In this game, you simply arrange to free-shape some specific behavior related to a box. Start with a cardboard box. But, you may decide to use different items for these games for a cat, a parrot, or a human child. First, decide on the target behavior. This might be pushing the box somewhere, standing in the box, picking up the box in the mouth/beak and bringing it to you or to some other location, or rolling the box over. After selecting a behavior, write out your approximation plan for that behavior. Remember, not too small, not too big. Then train the behavior.

When you have finished, contemplate the process and see if there is anything you could improve. Identify at least three things you could improve and how you will improve them.

Creativity Shaping Game

Glover and Gary (1976) formulated a game with human children that demonstrated the ability to condition creativity itself. Pryor and colleagues (1969) also conditioned creativity. We will use a box to play a shaping game designed specifically to condition creativity, incorporating elements of both of these research projects.

The creativity shaping game can be potentially frustrating and is intended for later stages in rehabilitation programs. It should be implemented for rehabilitative purposes only after a strong foundation of response-consequence contingency has been established and the subject is becoming empowered to a degree necessary to begin such an exercise!

In the creativity shaping game, your goal is to shape creativity itself, rather than a specific terminal behavior, as the reinforcement criterion. We will use a cardboard box. You may need to use another item to adapt this exercise to certain species. For instance, a paper towel roll can be used with parrots or cats. Simply present a cardboard box and wait for the subject to interact with it in some way. This might simply involve looking at the box or nudging it, for instance. When the subject does so, click and treat.

Reinforce this behavior three to five times so that it takes a foothold but has not developed a strong history of reinforcement. Then put that behavior on extinction. The subject's behavior will become variable. This will set the stage for the rest of the game by promoting interaction with the box generally.

In order to specifically implement a creativity component, establish a reinforcement criterion that involves different response class forms. For example, once the subject is reliably interacting with the box exhibiting the initial response class form, set the rule that through the next five responses to be reinforced there must be some other response class form. They may be somewhat similar, especially at first, but they must also be different in some way as well. If too few responses meeting the criterion occur, frustration should be prevented by arranging the environment in a way to encourage a different approach or otherwise a different behavior and allow slightly more similar response class forms to meet the reinforcement criterion. This will keep the conditioning on track and prevent frustration or boredom. When this is going smoothly, try another five reinforcement trials, again with a slightly different response class form being required. This training can be done as well with other objects in other environments to continue the generalization of creative and persistent responding.

Because you will be training creativity rather than a specific behavior, this can be challenging and potentially frustrating. Remember to keep up the enthusiasm and ensure that it does not become too frustrating. Shorter sessions are usually best for these kinds of training games.

You can set criteria to shape persistence in the same game, by requiring incrementally increased effort or attempts.

A Final Caution

Various means of rehabilitating depressed or disempowered responding in animals by training for empowerment—creativity, persistence/industriousness, and resilience have been explored. However, if the procedures in this book are implemented poorly, one could do more harm than good. Change itself can be stressful, and stress contributes to helplessness and depression. Furthermore, if carried out poorly or too hastily, some procedures discussed here—shaping and persistence training, in particular—can create stress and confusion, leading to further disempowerment.

It is *vital* that you maintain the primary objective during training! That is, remember that the goal is to set the subject up for success by managing the contingencies such that the subject does have to figure things out and keep plugging away in novel ways, but it is a fine line between creativity and persistence breakthroughs on the one hand, and frustration, confusion, and disempowerment, on the other. *Always* err on the side of setting the subject up for success! Proceed gradually and ensure that established contingencies remain stable. Start with very discrete creativity and persistence training sessions and generalize them incrementally.

Resources

Here are some potentially useful links:

Companion Animal Sciences Institute

Programs and courses in animal behavior:

http://www.casinstitute.com/

Association of Animal Behavior Professionals

A professional association for animal behavior technologists dedicated to noncoercive methods, a behavioral approach and professionalism:

http://www.associationofanimalbehaviorprofessionals.com/

Association of Animal Behavior Professionals Encyclopedic Glossary of Terms

http://www.associationofanimalbehaviorprofessionals.com/glossary.html

Bibliography

Bandura, A. (1977). Self-efficacy: Toward a unifying theory of behavioral change. *Psychological Review*, *84* (2), 191–215.

Bandura, A. (1982). Self-efficacy mechanism in human agency. *American Psychologist*, *37*(2), 122–147.

Branch, M. N. (2001). Are responses in avoidance procedures "safety" signals? *Journal of the Experimental Analysis of Behavior*, *75* (3), 351–354; discussion 367–378.

Brennan, F. X., Beck, K. D., & Servatius, R. J. (2003). Leverpress escape/avoidance conditioning in rats: safety signal length and avoidance performance. *Integrative Physiological and Behavioral Science*, *38* (1), 36–44.

Burch, M. R., & Bailey, J. S. (1999). *How Dogs Learn*. New York: Howell Book House.

Campbell, C. R., & Martinko, M. J. (1998). An integrative attributional perspective of empowerment and learned helplessness: A multimethod field study. *Journal of Management*, *24* (2), 173–200.

Chance, P. (2009). *Learning and behavior* (6th ed.). Belmont: Thomson Wadsworth.

Coburn, J. F., & Tarte, R. D. (1976). The effect of rearing environments on the contrafreeloading phenomenon in rats. *Journal of the Experimental Analysis of Behavior*, *26*, 289–294.

Cooper, J. O., Heron, T. E., & Heward, W. L. (2007). *Applied Behavior Analysis* (2nd ed.). Upper Saddle River: Merril Prentice Hall.

Deci, E. L., Koestner, R., & Ryan, R. M. (1999). The undermining effect is a reality after all—extrinsic rewards, task interest, and self-determination: Reply to Eisenberger, Pierce, and Cameron (1999) and Lepper, Henderlong, and Gingras (1999). *Psychological Bulletin*, *125* (6), 692–700.

de Jonge, F. H., Tilly, S., & Baars, A. M. (2008). On the rewarding nature of appetitive feeding behaviour in pigs (*Sus scrofa*): Do domesticated pigs contrafreeload? *Applied Animal Behaviour Science*, *114*, 359–372.

Delprato, D. J. (1981). The constructional approach to behavioral modification. *Journal of Behavior Therapy and Experimental Psychiatry*, *12* (1), 49–55.

Dinsmoor, J. A. (2001). Stimuli inevitably generated by behavior that avoids electric shock are inherently reinforcing. *Journal of the Experimental Analysis of Behavior*, *75* (3), 311–333.

Dougher, M. J., & Hackbert, L. (1994). A behavior-analytic account of depression and a case report using acceptance-based procedures. *The Behavior Analyst*, *17* (2), 321–334.

Dougher, M. J., & Hackbert, L. (2000). Establishing operations, cognition, and emotion. *The Behavior Analyst*, *23*(1), 11–24.

Drugan, R. C., Basile, A. S., Ha, J. H., Healy, D., & Ferland, R. J. (1997). Analysis of the importance of controllable versus uncontrollable stress on subsequent behavioral and physiological functioning. *Brain Research Protocols*, *2* (1), 69–74.

Eisenberger, R. (1992). Learned industriousness. *Psychological Review*, *99* (2), 248–267.

Eisenberger, R., & Armeli, S. (1997). Can salient reward increase creative performance without reducing intrinsic creative interest? *Journal of Personality and Social Psychology*, *72*(3), 652–663.

Eisenberger, R., Armeli, S., & Pretz, J. (1998). Can the promise of reward increase creativity? *Journal of Personality and Social Psychology*, *74* (3), 704–714.

Eisenberger, R., & Cameron, J. (1996). Detrimental effects of reward. *American Psychologist*, *51* (11), 1153–1166.

Eisenberger, R., & Leonard, J. M. (1980). Effects of conceptual task difficulty on generalized persistence. *American Journal of Psychology*, *93* (2), 285–298.

Eisenberger, R., Masterson, F. A., & McDermitt, M. (1982). Effects of task variety on generalized effort. *Journal of Educational Psychology*, *74* (4), 499–505.

Eisenberger, R., McDermitt, M., Masterson, F. A., & Over, S. (1983). Discriminative control of generalized effort. *American Journal of Psychology*, *96* (3), 353–364.

Ferster, C. B. (1973). A functional analysis of depression. *American Psychologist*, *28* (10), 857–870.

Fraley, L. (2008). *General Behaviorology: The Natural Science of Human Behavior*. Canton: ABCs.

Friedman, S. G. (2005). Empowering parrots. *Bird Talk*, *November*, 21–24.

Garcia, J., Ervin, F. R., & Koelling, R. A. (1966). Learning with prolonged delay of reinforcement. *Psychon. Sci*, *5* (3), 121–122.

Glover, J., & Gary, A. L. (1976). Procedures to increase some aspects of creativity. *Journal of Applied Behavior Analysis*, *9* (1), 79–84.

Goetz, E. M., & Baer, D. M. (1973). Social control of form diversity and the emergence of new forms in children's blockbuilding. *Journal of Applied Behavior Analysis*, *6* (2), 209–217.

Goldiamond, I. (2002). Toward a constructional approach to social problems: ethical and constitutional issues raised by applied behavior analysis. *Behavior and Social Issues*, *11*, 108–197. Retrieved September 12, 2005, from http://www.bfsr.org/BSI_11_2/11_2Gold.pdf

Herron, M. E., Schofer, F. S., & Reisner, I. R. (2009). Survey of the use and outcome of confrontational and non-confrontational training methods in client-owned dogs showing undesired behaviors. *Applied Animal Behaviour Science*, *117* (1–2), 47–54.

Inglis, I. R., Forkman, B., & Lazarus, J. (1997). Free food or earned food? A review and fuzzy model of contrafreeloading. *Animal Behaviour*, *53* (6), 1171–1191.

Job, R. F. (2002). The effects of uncontrollable, unpredictable aversive and appetitive events: similar effects warrant similar, but not identical, explanations? *Integrative Physiological and Behavioral Science*, *37* (1), 59–81.

Joels, M., Pu, Z., Wiegert, O., Oitzl, M. S., & Krugers, H. J. (2006). Learning under stress: how does it work? *Trends in Cognitive Sciences*, *10* (4), 152–158.

Kanter, J. W., Busch, A. M., Weeks, C. E., & Landes, S. J. (2008). The nature of clinical depression: Symptoms, syndromes, and behavior analysis. *The Behavior Analyst*, *31* (1), 1–21.

Klein, D. C., Fencil-Morse, E., & Seligman, M. E. (1976). Learned helplessness, depression, and the attribution of failure. *Journal of Personality and Social Psychology*, *33* (5), 508–516.

Klein, D. C., & Seligman, M. E. (1976). Reversal of performance deficits and perceptual deficits in learned helplessness and depression. *Journal of Abnormal Psychology*, *85* (1), 11–26.

Kodak, T., Lerman, D. C., Volkert, V. M., & Trosclair, N. (2007). Further examination of factors that influence preference for positive versus negative reinforcement. *Journal of Applied Behavior Analysis*, *40* (1), 25–44.

Kodak, T., Miltenberger, R. G., & Romaniuk, C. (2003). The effects of differential negative reinforcement of other behavior and noncontingent escape on compliance. *Journal of Applied Behavior Analysis*, *36* (3), 379–382.

Koelen, M. A., & Lindstrom, B. (2005). Making healthy choices easy choices: the role of empowerment. *European Journal of Clinical Nutrition*, *59* (Suppl 1), S10–S16.

Langer, E. J. (1975). The illusion of control. *Journal of Personality and Social Psychology*, *32* (2), 331–328.

Lattal, K. A., Reilly, M. P., & Kohn, J. P. (1998). Response persistence under ratio and interval reinforcement schedules. *Journal of the Experimental Analysis of Behavior, 70*, 165–183.

Leone, C., & Burns, J. (2000). The measurement of locus of control: assessing more than meets the eye? *Journal of Psychology, 134* (1), 63–76.

Lerman, D. C., Iwata, B. A., Shore, B. A., & Kahng, S. W. (1996). Responding maintained by intermittent reinforcement: implications for the use of extinction with problem behavior in clinical settings. *Journal of Applied Behavior Analysis, 29* (2), 153–171.

Levis, D. J. (1976). Learned helplessness: A reply and alternative S-R interpretation. *Journal of Experimental Psychology: General, 105* (1), 47–65.

Maier, S. F., & Warren, D. A. (1988). Controllability and safety signals exert dissimilar proactive effects on nociception and escape performance. *Journal of Experimental Psychology: Animal Behavior Processes, 14* (1), 18–25.

Maldonado, A. (2002). Research on irrelevance, helplessness, and immunization against helplessness in Spain: past, present, and future. *Integrative Physiological and Behavioral Science, 37* (1), 22–34.

Malone, J. C. (1975). Stimulus-specific contrast effects during operant discrimination learning. *Journal of the Experimental Analysis of Behavior, 24* (3), 281–289.

Miltenberger, R. G. (2008). *Behavior Modification Principles and Procedures* (4th ed.). Belmont: Thomson Wadsworth.

Monfils, M. H., Cowansage, K. K., Klann, E., & LeDoux, J. E. (2009). Extinction-reconsolidation boundaries: key to persistent attenuation of fear memories. *Science, 324* (5929), 951–955.

Moore, J. (2008). Conceptual Foundations of Radical Behaviorism. Cornwall-on-Hudson, Sloan Publishing.

Mowrer, O. H., & Viek, P. (1948). An experimental analogue of fear from a sense of helplessness. *Journal of Abnormal Psychology, 43* (2), 193–200.

Munera, J. (2008–2009), Solitary or social? Social organization of the domestic cat. *New College Academic Journal, (3)*, 12–13.

Nation, J. R., Cooney, J. B., & Gartrell, K. E. (1979). Durability and generalizability of persistence training. *Journal of Abnormal Psychology, 88* (2), 121–136.

Nation, J. R., & Massad, P. (1978). Persistence training: a partial reinforcement procedure for reversing learned helplessness and depression. *Journal of Experimental Psychology: General, 107* (4), 436–451.

Nation, J. R., & Woods, D. J. (1980). Persistence: The role of partial reinforcement in psychotherapy. *Journal of Experimental Psychology: General, 109* (2), 175–207.

Nevin, J. (1996). The momentum of compliance. *Journal of Applied Behavior Analysis, 29* (4), 535–547.

Nevin, J. A., Mandell, C., & Atak, J. R. (1983). The analysis of behavioral momentum. *Journal of the Experimental Analysis of Behavior, 39* (1), 49–59.

Nyatanga, L., & Dann, K. L. (2002). Empowerment in nursing: the role of philosophical and psychological factors. *Nursing Philosophy, 3*, 234–239.

O'Heare, J. (2008). *Dominance Theory and Dogs* (2nd ed.). Ottawa: Dogpsych Publishing.

O'Heare, J. (2009a). The least intrusive effective behavior intervention (LIEBI) algorithm and levels of intrusiveness table: A proposed best-practices model. *Journal of Applied Companion Animal Behavior, 3* (1), 7–25.

O'Heare, J. (2009b). *Separation Distress and Dogs*. Ottawa: BehaveTech Publishing.

O'Heare, J. (2010). *Changing problem behavior*. Ottawa: BehaveTech Publishing.

O'Heare, J. (2018a). *Resolving Fears, Phobias, and Anxieties: A Guide for Dog Guardians*. Ottawa, Canada: BehaveTech Publishing.

O'Heare, J. (2018b). *Resolving Fears, Phobias, and Anxieties: An Errorless Differential Reinforcement Approach for Professionals*. Ottawa, Canada: BehaveTech Publishing.

O'Neill, R. E., Horner, R. H., Albin, R. W., Sprague, J. R., Storey, K., & Newton, J. S. (1997). *Functional Assessment and Program Development for Problem Behavior A Practical Handbook*. New York: Brooks/Cole Publishing Company.

Overmier, J. B. (2002). On learned helplessness. *Integrative Physiological and Behavioral Science*, *37* (1), 4–8.

Overmier, J. B., & Seligman, M. E. (1967). Effects of inescapable shock upon subsequent escape and avoidance responding. *Journal of Comparative and Physiological Psychology*, *63*, 28–33.

Pigg, K. E. (2002). Three faces of empowerment: Expanding the theory of empowerment in community development. *Journal of the Community Development Society*, *107* (17).

Plaud, J. J., & Gaither, G. A. (1996). Human behavioral momentum: Implications for applied behavior analysis and therapy. *Journal of Behavior Therapy and Experimental Psychiatry*, *27* (2), 139–148.

Prilleltensky, I., Nelson, G., & Peison, L. (2001). The role of power and control in children's lives: An ecological analysis of pathways toward wellness, resilience and problems. *Journal of Community and Applied Social Psychology*, *11*, 143–158.

Pryor, K. (1999). *Don't shoot the dog! The new art of teaching and training*. New York: Bantom Books.

Pryor, K. (2009). 101 things to do with a box. Retrieved from http://www.clickertraining.com/node/167

Pryor, K. W., Haag, R., & O'Reilly, J. (1969). The creative porpoise: training for novel behavior. *Journal of the Experimental Analysis of Behavior*, *12* (4), 653–661.

Rescorla, R. A. (1969). Establishment of a positive reinforcer through contrast with shock. *Journal of Comparative and Physiological Psychology*, *67* (2), 260–263.

Richter, C. P. (1957). On the phenomenon of sudden death in animals and man. *Psychosomatic Medicine*, *19*(3), 191–198.

Robbins, D. (1971). Partial reinforcement: A selective review of the alleyway literature since 1960. *Psychological Bulletin*, *76* (6), 415–431.

Rosellini, R. A., & Seligman, M. E. (1975). Frustration and learned helplessness. *Journal of Experimental Psychology: Animal Behavior Processes*, *1* (2), 149–157.

Seligman, M. E. (1990/1998). *Learned Optimism: How to Change Your Mind and Your Life*. New York: Pocket Books.

Seligman, M. E., & Maier, S. F. (1967). Failure to escape traumatic shock. *Journal of Experimental Psychology*, *74* (1), 1–9.

Seligman, M. E., Maier, S. F., & Geer, J. H. (1968). Alleviation of learned helplessness in the dog. *Journal of Abnormal Psychology*, *73* (3), 256–262.

Seligman, M. E., Rosellini, R. A., & Kozak, M. J. (1975). Learned helplessness in the rat: time course, immunization, and reversibility. *Journal of Comparative and Physiological Psychology*, *88* (2), 542–547.

Shull, R. L., & Grimes, J. A. (2006). Resistance to extinction following variable-interval reinforcement: Reinforcer rate and amount. *Journal of the Experimental Analysis of Behavior*, *85*, 23–39.

Sidman, M. (2001). *Coercion and its fallout* (Revised ed.). Boston: Author's Cooperative, Inc. Publishers.

Smith, S. M., & Davis, E. S. (2007). Clicker increases resistance to extinction but does not decrease training time of a simple operant task in domestic dogs (*Canis familiaris*). *Applied Animal Behaviour Science*, *110* (3–4), 318–329.

Starr, M. D., & Mineka, S. (1977). Determinants of fear over the course of avoidance learning. *Learning and Motivation*, *8*, 332–350.

Terrace, H. S. (1974). On the nature of non-responding in discrimination learning with and without errors. *Journal of the Experimental Analysis of Behavior*, *22* (1), 151–159.

Udell, M. A., & Wynne, C. D. (2008). A review of domestic dogs' (*Canis familiaris*) human-like behaviors: or why behavior analysts should stop worrying and love their dogs. *Journal of the Experimental Analysis of Behavior*, *89* (2), 247–261.

Volpicelli, J. R., Ulm, R. R., Altenor, A., & Seligman, M. E. P. (1983). Learned mastery in the rat. *Learning and Motivation*, *14*, 204–222.

Voith, V. L. (1977). Aggressive behavior and dominance. *Canine Practice*, April, 8–15.

Wikipedia.org (2009). Self-efficacy. Retrieved November 19, 2009, from http://en.wikipedia.org/wiki/Self-efficacy

Wong, P. T. P. (1979). Frustration, exploration, and learning. *Canadian Psychological Review*, *20* (3), 133–144.

Wood, L. (n.d.). Clicker bridging stimulus efficacy. Retrieved from http://www.clickertraining.com/files/Wood_Lindsay_CLICKER_BRIDGING_STIMULUS_EFFICACY.pdf

Woods, A. M., & Bouton, M. E. (2007). Occasional reinforced responses during extinction can slow the rate of reacquisition of an operant response. *Learning and Motivation*, *38* (1), 56–74.